C000053247

Rise and Inspire

Find Your Voice, Tell Your Story, and Share Your Message as a Speaker

David McCrae

Copyright © 2021 David McCrae

David McCrae has asserted his right to be identified as the author of this work in accordance with the Copyright, Designs and Patents Act 1998.

All rights reserved. No part of this book may be reproduced by any mechanical, photographic, or electronic process, or in the form of a phonographic recording; nor may it be stored in a retrieval system, transmitted, or otherwise copied for public or private use — other than for "fair use" as brief quotations embodied in articles and reviews — without prior written permission of the author.

Every effort has been made to ensure that details for websites and links are up to date at the time of publishing. The author takes no responsibility for links that are changed or removed after publication.

This book describes a variety of outcomes and results. Please remember that individual results applying the information in this book will vary. The author provides no guarantee of any results you might achieve from reading this book, whether they be financial, professional, social or any other word ending in "-al". The beauty of speaking is that it is such a personal journey and whilst you won't be able to replicate anyone else, no one will be able to replicate you.

Cover Design: Mercedes Pinera
Paperback ISBN: 9798587193055
1st Edition, February 2021

In memory of my dad, Jim McCrae, who is the reason why I stand on stage.
(21/07/1939 - 24/07/2015)

This book is dedicated to Brendon Burchard, who convinced me it was possible.

Contents

Prologue: Take Your Seats

"But while I may be the first woman in this office, I won't be the last. Because every little girl watching tonight sees that this is a country of possibilities."

"And to the children of our country, regardless of your gender, our country has sent you a clear message: Dream with ambition, lead with conviction, and see yourself in a way that others might not see you, simply because they've never seen it before."

(Kamala Harris. Vice Presidential Acceptance Speech, 2020.)

He stands on stage, faces stretching towards the back of the hotel ballroom. All eight hundred people have their eyes closed as he takes his audience through one final visualisation exercise.

Four days of work have culminated in this moment. One final chance to impart his desired message to the audience. Over twenty-five hours of speaking and this could decide whether his students go on to implement what they have learned.

As the visualisation becomes more emotional, one of those eight hundred people bursts into tears.

It's a twenty-three-year-old man, who has traveled twenty-seven hours across half the world to be at this event, hoping to find out who he is and what he's supposed to do in life.

That young man is me.

In 2016, I traveled from my home country of Scotland to San Jose, California, to try and find my purpose.

I had lost my dad to cancer nine months earlier and I was trying to find my way in life after this loss.

I had placed my faith in this man on stage to help me.

His name was Brendon Burchard and this event was Experts Academy, a four-day seminar where people learn how to share their story and experience to educate and inspire others.

On that final day, I burst into tears because I finally realised something.

I finally realised I was capable of something.

To look at me from the outside, this wouldn't have been a surprise. I had a degree in Psychology from one of the top five psychology schools in the United Kingdom. During my time at university, I had served as the President of the Student Psychology Society and also published two novels. I would definitely have been labeled a 'high-performer'. There was potential to enjoy a prestigious career and earn a decent salary as an academic or researcher.

I didn't cry that day because I realised I was capable of a prestigious career and a decent salary. I didn't care about that.

I didn't want to hide away in a research lab and publish papers. I didn't want to accumulate letters after my name. I didn't want to settle for a comfortable paycheck.

I studied psychology firstly to try and make sense of my own challenges and secondly to help other people do the same.

Like many idealistic youths, I wanted to make a difference.

I turned my back on academia and looked for a different route to making an impact.

My attendance at Experts Academy was part of this journey.

I burst into tears not because I realised I would be a good academic: I burst into tears because I realised I was capable of so much more.

For the first time in my life, I realised what I was truly capable of.

Not capable of getting good grades at school. Not capable of getting a nice house. Not capable of settling down and starting a family.

I realised I was capable of changing people's lives and it was now time to start making the most of my abilities.

With tears running down my face, I smiled.

I now knew what my purpose was.

At that moment, I experienced the power of speaking. I was getting a first-hand account of the difference it could make.

I couldn't believe how much just standing on stage and talking could change someone's life. As the visualisation ended and I looked around at my fellow students, I saw I wasn't the only one crying.

I knew at that moment that my purpose was to be a speaker. I saw how I could make a difference. To one day move and inspire someone the way that Brendon had moved and inspired me.

It was time for me to Rise and Inspire.

Introduction: Housekeeping

"Now in fact, some of our transformative leaders in history have been introverts. I'll give you some examples. Eleanor Roosevelt, Rosa Parks, Gandhi —all these people described themselves as quiet and soft-spoken and even shy."

"And they all took the spotlight, even though every bone in their bodies was telling them not to. And this turns out to have a special power all its own, because people could feel that these leaders were at the helm not because they enjoyed directing others and not out of the pleasure of being looked at; they were there because they had no choice, because they were driven to do what they thought was right."

(Susan Cain. TED: Long Beach California, 2012.)

It's time for you too to Rise and Inspire. It's time for you to fulfil your purpose.

You have a message to share and there has been no better time in history to share it.

The world is connecting like never before. You can already broadcast a message to anyone, anywhere, anytime: plus it's easy and free to do so. You can run your own publishing service on Amazon, your own radio show on Apple Podcasts and your own television show on Youtube.

What is even more exciting is that the scope to do so is increasing year upon year. Over 50% of the world are connected to the internet. You can reach people who have never heard of you before, in places you have never heard of before.

Speaking is an ability we all have, you do it every day. You can make the most of that ability.

If you improve your public speaking then you can inspire and impact the lives of hundreds or thousands of people at a time.

With public speaking you can promote your creative talent, reach new customers and boost your profit.

Public speaking even just changes you as a person. It develops confidence and improves your ability to face your challenges and fears. Furthermore, as you enhance your communication on-stage, you also enhance your ability to communicate off-stage in your everyday interactions.

Yet, even though you have a message to share, you maybe don't know how. Perhaps you are scared to try, or don't believe that you're good enough.

Public speaking is our number one fear and quite frankly we have never been taught how to do it. Your confidence and your competence in this area is low.

The only speakers you have seen on stage or on Youtube are brilliant, possessing confidence and skill that you can't imagine having.

Additionally, you've maybe noticed that most successful speakers seem to be old, white dudes in suits and so you've placed the limitation on yourself that you're too young/female/tanned to be a speaker. (and yes, I'm aware of my hypocrisy/privilege that I will one day be an old, white dude, definitely not in a suit though).

These speakers all started from a place very far from excellence. It's where we all start as speakers.

When I made that decision to be a speaker, I was twenty-three years old and didn't have a clue what I was doing.

I was running events in any cheap venue I could find: pubs, coffee shops, community centres.

I was emailing anyone who I thought might let me do a workshop for them: schools, charities, businesses.

I took whatever small opportunity I could and started to build belief and momentum for myself.

Six months after Experts Academy — a month before I turned twenty-four — I ran my first full-day seminar. Twenty-one people bought tickets and through selling some coaching I managed to make £600 in a single day. That was more than I had earned in entire months in my student jobs.

On that day I felt so aligned and connected to what I was doing. I knew I had found what I was meant to do.

I started to run more of these events, learning how to create better content and market more effectively.

I began running multiple events a month in multiple cities. In July 2019 this culminated in my first two-day event, speaking for sixteen hours and building towards one day running an event like Experts Academy.

Throughout this journey, I have been a member of Toastmasters International, a worldwide organisation dedicated to helping its members improve their public speaking and leadership skills. In 2019, I was crowned the Scottish Champion in the Toastmasters Speech Evaluation Contest and elected President of my Toastmasters club.

This journey has not been a smooth one, however. I have run plenty of events where I didn't connect properly with the audience and people left before the event was over, or as soon as I had finished talking. I have got my marketing strategy wrong and got a poor turnout, or not spoken to my ideal audience. I have lost money on a number of events due to this lack of connection or poor turnout. I have lost as many speech contests as I have won.

Nonetheless, there are valuable lessons to take from both good and bad events. Through this process I have learned what works and what doesn't work, especially when starting out.

So many people think that in order to start out, they need a high level of speaking ability and professional credibility. They wait to 'get' these, without realising that this is exactly what you develop through the process of speaking! You don't need either to start.

Don't get me wrong, you do need to be able to communicate a message and you do need to have integrity in how you communicate it. What you don't need are the oratory skills of Martin Luther King or the credentials of Stephen Hawking to be able to make a difference.

We've all been to an event with someone who was very charismatic, but we didn't really connect to them and even felt they were a bit false. Alternatively, we've also been to an event where the speaker clearly knew their stuff but bored us to tears. Being a good speaker or possessing a lot of knowledge does not guarantee your success.

What really matters in the beginning is your effort and your authenticity. If you show you care, people will care. All I built my success on was a story and a degree and, to be honest, no-one usually asks about the degree.

All you need, not just to get started, but to make an impact, is a message and a platform. In this book you will learn how to build both.

In the first section, Rise, you will learn the 3M framework of Mindset, Message and Mastery, that will help you cultivate confidence, find your purpose, and develop your unique speaking skills.

In the second section, Inspire, you will learn the ABC Framework of Audience, Business and Content that will help you build a loyal following, transmit your message and get you on stages.

There has never been a better time in history than right now to become a speaker and share your message. You are able to reach people who need to hear what you have to say.

You are almost certainly in a better position than I was starting out. You will have more expertise and/or life experience than I did at twenty-three. If I can make it, you can too. Becoming a speaker is not complicated, it just takes time to build and improve. In this book you will learn what you need to do.

If you have the drive and vision to impact others, you will be a successful speaker. If you care and give a damn, that shows, and the people who need your wisdom will resonate with you.

The world needs more people like you who have something of value to share. The world has too many people broadcasting negativity. People like us need to speak up and make our voices heard.

It's time for you to Rise and Inspire.

Chapter 1: Rise Of The Speaker

"Many people say that Sweden is just a small country and it doesn't matter what we do. But I've learnt that no one is too small to make a difference."

"And if a few children can get headlines all over the world just by not going to school — then imagine what we all could do together if we really wanted to."

(Greta Thunberg. UN Climate Change Conference, 2018.)

I have already stated that there has never been a better time to get into the world of speaking. That is because I believe that the field of speaking is still relatively in its infancy.

On the one hand, humans have been delivering speeches for thousands of years. Greeks philosophised in the amphitheatre. Romans debated in the Senate. Christians preached in the churches.

In more recent times there has been the Gettysburg Address, 'We choose to go to the Moon' and 'Yes We Can'.

On the other hand, the idea of speaking as a profession is still relatively new.

Most of the time, speaking has been attached to other roles and duties such as academia, business, and politics.

Because of this, speaking has been dominated by those folks we were talking about earlier, the old white dudes in suits. Only a small proportion of the world's population has been taking the stage.

Not only has speaking been limited in terms of who is doing it, but it has also been limited in terms of the way we have approached it.

Most speaking has fallen into two camps.

Informational: trying to tell someone something
Motivational: trying to get someone to do something

Generally, speakers are only proficient in one of these two areas. They have good content but poor delivery. Alternatively, they have a strong delivery but little of substance to say. They are wise or charismatic. We've had to choose between breathtaking and banal.

Speakers can do far better than this and we're going to see everything change as we advance further into the 21st century.

Those old white dudes are going to die (and I'm going to become one of them!). The old will be replaced by the young. The white will be replaced with black. The dudes will be replaced with ladies. The suits will be replaced with hijabs.

The opportunity, and necessity, to speak will rise. No longer will stages be reserved for academics, businessmen, and politicians. Everyday people will be given the stage and will need to learn how to make the most of this opportunity.

Speaking will move away from traditional, established platforms, down to grassroots level.

We need to prepare for this evolution and I think we have a lot of catching up to do.

As it stands, most people are not taught to speak on stage. Our school systems brush over it and any such training is often conducted in a wooden, rehearsed manner. We produce children who rely on notes and rote memory to speak on stage when children are the most natural speakers in the world off the stage.

Any speakers we develop are generally one-dimensional. They have content or delivery: rarely both. They are either competent or confident: rarely both.

We need to teach people how to express themselves with conviction; to be able to speak to both the head and the heart and possess both substance and style.

This is not too much to ask. There is only a small shift that is required.

We are all effective communicators... we do it in conversations every day. When we step up on stage we seem to forget how we communicate day-to-day. We will become much better speakers when we recognise that the stage is just an enhanced conversation.

We get taught these stiff, over-practiced ways to speak. We get taught to memorise our lines and stuff our PowerPoints with text in case we forget. How many conversations have you needed to rehearse or needed a PowerPoint to conduct? If you spoke in real life like so many of us end up speaking on stage, you would never connect with anyone.

We get taught this artificial model of what a speaker should look and sound like, leaving no scope for personal flair and expression. We need to stop speaking like speakers and start speaking like us.

This is why when we speak we get stuck in our head. We get stuck on what to say next, how to say it, and what the audience thinks about us. If you stay stuck in your head, you will never truly connect with people. Humans connect heart to heart, not head to head.

When we know our stuff, there is no need to stay stuck in our heads. You don't need the rehearsal, the PowerPoints, and the stock speaker mannerisms. Express what you know through the heart and people will connect with it.

You will become a powerful speaker if you can develop a synergy between styles. If you can be both informational and motivational; both competent and confident.

Imagine if we could make this small shift. If we could create a generation of speakers who communicated with conviction.

There would be classrooms and lecture theatres that are no longer filled with disengaged students.

There would be workplace presentations that don't inflict death by PowerPoint and actually create the change they are intended to.

There would be politicians we could resonate with and look up to. (okay, maybe I'm being a little optimistic on that one!)

People will have more freedom and confidence to express who they really are, not just on stage but throughout their lives.

We will live in a world of more effective communicators. We will resolve our conflicts and collaborate better.

We will see more people who Rise and Inspire.

Chapter 2: My Rise

"I think what we've learned is that, if you're a teacher, your words can be meaningful, but if you're a compassionate teacher, they can be especially meaningful."

"When we create the right kind of identity, we can say things to the world around us that they don't actually believe make sense. We can get them to do things that they don't think they can do."

(Bryan Stevenson. TED: Long Beach California, 2012.)

I had delivered presentations at school and university but I don't count these as public speaking. I was delivering a rehearsed script or elaborating on a PowerPoint. I was speaking about trivialities such as my favourite film or the three parts of the Cognitive Triad.

The first time I truly stepped up and delivered something meaningful was at my dad's funeral.

If you have read my previous books, you will know that the loss of my dad at age twenty-two was a huge catalyst and wake-up call for me. It would drive me on to become the author and speaker I am today.

However, at that point, I had no foresight as to where I was going to end up. All I knew was that there was a funeral to organise and someone had to deliver it.

I knew that I didn't want someone who had never met Dad to get on stage and try to summarise his life. I didn't want another family member who thought they knew Dad to get on stage and mess it up. Towards the end of his life, I knew Dad better than anyone: I knew that if Dad was to get the send-off he deserved, I would have to be the one to do it.

I spent a week writing a eulogy, practicing it, and refining it. Getting the poignancy and humour just right. Working out what impression I wanted to leave on the audience. Working out what was most important to say about Dad.

I was nervous as people took their seats. I didn't know whether I could stay composed during the reading. I had cried several times during the rehearsals and that was in the privacy of solitude. Now I had to do it with the pressure of people's grief and expectations.

For twenty minutes I held it together. I didn't flub a line. I landed my jokes. I brought my eulogy to a close and I instructed the audience to stand. Dad didn't like the minute's silence that is often held for deceased public figures. He much preferred it when there was a minute's applause instead. I led that one minute's applause and we sent Dad off in the way that he deserved.

Dad's brother-in-law approached me after the ceremony and told me it was the best eulogy he had ever heard. My Dad's best friend said he had been mesmerised. In the most difficult of circumstances, I had discovered my ability as a speaker.

Even with that feedback, I didn't think much more about my speaking ability. The initial months after Dad's death was just a case of survival, trying to come to terms with life without a loved one. As the grief eased, I started to look into the world of coaching and online courses, feeling that I might have something to offer in this regard.

This is what took me to Experts Academy nine months after Dad's death. It was here that I realised that my purpose was to be a speaker. That I could use that ability for more than just honouring loved ones. I could help the people still alive.

I am a big fan of starting before you are ready in life. I have done that with almost every major endeavour. I left home before I was ready. I worked abroad before I was ready. I started writing books before I was ready. I also started speaking before I was ready.

I started with a two-hour workshop on a Friday night. I rented the cheapest room I could get at my old university. I printed out 1,000 flyers and walked around the surrounding area and personally posted each one through a letterbox.

I managed to get fifteen people to attend that workshop, almost half of whom were friends who came along as a favour to me. It didn't matter though. I got in the game.

I started a Meetup group and organised more events. In the beginning, I was running workshops for four people in a pub basement, the only venue I could find that would let me hire a space for free. There was no door between the basement and the bar area, so the music and drunken banter from upstairs was making as much noise as I was.

A sympathetic coffee shop owner let me hire his upstairs space after closing time for £10 an hour. The first workshop I ran in that space had a grand audience of three people.

I called and emailed schools, universities, charities, businesses, and Meetup groups to try to get any gig I could. A mental health charity let me run a workshop in the backroom of a church for twelve people. A networking group let me do a five-minute pitch on the top floor of a pub. A goal-setting Meetup group let me do a fifteen-minute keynote in a community hall.

These were small opportunities but they got me in the game and I started to build belief and momentum for myself.

Desperate to take things further, I escalated my commitment and decided to run my first full-day event. I wanted to emulate, on a smaller scale, Experts Academy and the deep immersive experience that had changed me.

The seminar was called 'Curriculum for Fulfilment' and I decided to teach three subjects that were of interest to me and I thought were beneficial for people to know more about: psychology, personal development, and relationships. I set a date and booked the room, giving myself 30 days to create and market the event.

I had no idea what to charge for such an event and I was also worried that no one would come. Therefore, I decided to ask people to pay for the ticket with a donation; whatever they thought the event might be worth.

I went to every networking and Meetup group I could and ran some Facebook ads. In the four weeks leading up to the event, I sold twenty-one tickets, with donations ranging from £1 (of course) to £50. Sixteen of those students showed up, and I spent a day with them teaching, playing games, and engaging in reflective activities. I loved every moment. I had, whether through luck or skill, managed to assemble a positive and engaged set of students and it was a pleasure to spend the day with them.

I pitched some coaching at the end of the seminar and had two of those sixteen sign up. When I combined the ticket sales and the coaching, I had managed to earn £600 ($900) with one event. Now that was not a single day's work, as it had taken a whole month to prepare and promote the seminar, but I could see the promise and potential of speaking. I was just about to turn twenty-four, and I knew I had a lot of time ahead of me to master and fulfil this purpose.

I had enjoyed success with this seminar but I was still struggling to make speaking a regular thing. I still had those small workshops and occasional free gig, but little else. I had poured my heart and soul into 'Curriculum For Fulfilment' and trying to replicate that consistently was unfeasible.

That changed when, a couple of months later, I published my third book, my first self-help book: *The Last 60 Minutes*. This book covered the experience of losing Dad and the lessons I had learned from his death. Within a week of publication, it hit #1 on Amazon in the Death and Grief category.

This book suddenly acted like a magic calling card. I couldn't believe how many more times I was offered speaking opportunities just because I now had a book. I managed to get onto BBC radio to speak about the book. I was invited to events in other cities across the UK to share the story and message of the book.

My audiences started to grow for the events I ran too. I upgraded from coffee shops and community halls to hotel meeting rooms. I could present on TV screens rather than whiteboards stuck to the wall. The audience could sit on soft cushions rather than biting wood or plastic. There was even central heating now!

In 2018 I organised my very first book tour for my fourth book *Author Your Life: Become the Hero of Your Story*, running events in four different cities across the UK.

In 2019 I ran my very first multi-day event. The same year I won my first national award for speaking. It's a far cry from competing with the pub jukebox.

Becoming a speaker was about two things: connecting with my why and getting in the game. Once I knew it was my purpose to be a speaker, nothing was going to stop me. I spoke in those pubs and community halls because I knew that was what was required to advance.

The same will be true for you too. When you know in your heart that you are meant to be a speaker and know why your message is so important, that will drive you on through all the graft required. It will drive you on through all the initiation and learning until you get to the point where you too, will Rise and Inspire.

Chapter 3: Your Rise

"Women are very slow to rouse, but once they are aroused, once they are determined, nothing on Earth and nothing in heaven will make women give way; it is impossible."

(Emmeline Pankhurst. 'Freedom or Death', 1913.)

How can you also Rise and Inspire? As you are reading this book, you probably haven't stepped into that role as you would like to. You are looking to reach more people with your message. You have creative talents that aren't being fully utilised. You aren't making the money you want to.

The first challenge that aspiring speakers encounter is the "who am I?" voice in their head.

Who am I to express myself?

Who am I to share an opinion?

Who am I to lead others?

Sound familiar?

It's the insidious voice of doubt and it's a great thing that you have it.

Yes, really.

You'll learn why later in the book.

The second challenge that aspiring speakers confront is "where do I even begin?"

You've felt that tug in your heart to become a speaker.

You've heard the call of the stage.

You realise you have a duty and responsibility to change the lives of others.

Now what?

What is my purpose as a speaker?

Where is my journey taking me?

You'll be surprised at the answers you find later in this book.

The third challenge aspiring speakers overcome is "how do I do this?"

How do I become a better speaker?

How do I inspire people with what I say?

When you start your journey, you are very aware that you're not especially good at this.

That's okay because you are starting just where everyone else does.

In this book, you will learn what it takes to get off the start line.

In the first section of this book, 'Rise', we will examine how you develop yourself as a speaker. We will explore this through the 3M framework.

The first step is **Mindset.** You're going to learn how to break through the voices in your head so that you can find the voice in your heart and speak it with confidence.

The second step is **Message.** You are going to clarify what you speak on and who your audience is so that you can make the impact you desire as a speaker.

The third step is **Mastery.** You will learn how to develop your speaking style and skill so that you can speak effortlessly and authentically.

Stepping into our role as a speaker and rising is great...but it's just the first step.

Being a fantastic speaker is only part of the equation.

Who is your ideal audience? Fantastic speaking abilities are severely blunted if you aren't speaking in front of the right people.

What do you need to do to earn money? You need more than a sharp tongue to keep a roof over your head and food in your belly.

How do you create engaging content? There's no point in being articulate if what you are saying doesn't appeal to the audience.

This is the business of speaking. You need to know how to get your message out into the world. That is why the title is Rise AND Inspire.

'Inspire' is therefore the second section of this book and this is where you are going to learn how to sustain and grow your message. We will accomplish this through the ABC framework.

The first step is **Audience.** You will learn how to reach the people who most need to hear your message and build a loyal following.

The second step is **Business.** You will learn how to build the structure of a successful speaking business so that you are thinking about your mission rather than worrying about money.

The third step is **Content.** You will learn how to create and structure your speeches to make them compelling to this ideal audience.

These two sections are going to take you on a journey. A journey to build you up as the speaker you are capable of being and having the impact you are capable of having.

Through these frameworks, you will Rise and Inspire.

Section 1: Rise

"All I know is that I care about this problem, and I want to make it better. And, having seen what I've seen, and given the chance, I feel it is my responsibility to say something."

"Statesman Edmund Burke said, 'All that is needed for the forces of evil to triumph is for good men and women to do nothing.'"

"In my nervousness for this speech and in my moments of doubt, I told myself firmly, 'If not me, who? If not now, when?'"

(Emma Watson. 'HeForShe': United Nations, 2014.)

When you first begin on the path to becoming an inspirational speaker, you start with a lot of passion and enthusiasm, but not much else. You feel an urge to inspire, but you don't really know how you're going to go about doing that.

That is why this book is called Rise and Inspire. You must first Rise before you can Inspire. You must stand up with confidence and conviction in your story and message so that you can Inspire others with what you have to share.

The next three chapters are going to help you do this.

Chapter 4 is entitled '**Mindset**'. In this chapter you will learn how to build a mindset that helps you feel clear and confident in your role as a speaker. You will do this by learning:

- Why speaking is similar to driving
- The difference between "I do" and "I am"
- What to start collecting as soon as you begin speaking
- The fine tightrope your idols will make you walk
- The pronoun you need to swap
- The four step journey to building confidence

Chapter 5 is entitled '**Message**'. In this chapter you are going to find clarity on what your message is and who you are going to deliver it to. You will do this by learning:

- That pain is a good thing
- The importance of answering the right questions
- That six minutes of speaking is surprisingly revealing
- The four different types of speaker

Chapter 6 is entitled '**Mastery**'. In this chapter you will learn how to build your skill and unlock your natural expression as a speaker. You will do this by learning:

- Why you should approach speaking like you approach yoga
- Why Croatia is better than Scotland (and I'm Scottish)
- How pretending I was a pole dancer helped me win a national speaking championship
- That you can already teach people how to be better public speakers (and why you should)

In these chapters you are going to learn how to Rise as a speaker. How to become the inspiration that you are capable of being.

This sets you up for the second section of this book, which is **'Inspire'**. In this section you will take everything you have learned and worked on in this first section and start using it to build your audience and make your difference to their lives.

No skipping ahead to the sexy part first though! Read the next three chapters and build your foundations as a speaker, and Rise into the speaker you are capable of being.

Chapter 4: Mindset

"And so I want to say to you, don't fake it till you make it. Fake it till you become it. Do it enough until you actually become it and internalise."

(Amy Cuddy. TED: Edinburgh, 2012.)

Before we go any further, there is a very important question I have to ask.

Do you want to be a speaker?

I'm not asking this as a form of rah-rah affirmation, to get you pumped up or saying "yes" to what I tell you.

I'm asking you this question because you need to think about the answer and prepare for the work required and the responsibility you take on if you become a speaker.

Watching a TED talk or going to a Tony Robbins seminar might make speaking seem very glamorous and an alternative to a rockstar lifestyle if you have no musical talent.

But like all snapshots of success, you are just seeing the finalised 1%.

Are you willing to take on the other 99% of the journey?

My account of my speaking journey earlier on may have seemed romantic and poetic, but it wasn't.

Are you prepared to spend evenings and weekends scripting speeches and making slides?

Are you prepared to spend days practicing your timings and refining your content?

Are you prepared to speak to audiences that you could fit into your living room?

Are you prepared to speak to disinterested, rude or hostile audiences?

Are you prepared to spend hours filming videos that no one watches when you post them online?

Are you prepared to doubt yourself and to question why you're even bothering?

That is the reality not just when you begin speaking, but what continues to happen after years of doing it.

You need to be prepared for that and frankly most prospective speakers are not.

They are not prepared for the dedication and effort this path takes.

This is why I ask, with utmost sincerity, whether you really want to be a speaker.

At Experts Academy, I realised my purpose was to be a speaker, and I wasn't going to stop until I had fulfilled that purpose. One of my strengths is that when I set my mind to something, I make it happen.

You need to have that type of psychology.

To get up on stage or onto camera again and again.

To spend hundreds of hours refining your craft.

And that's just to get into the game, never mind make the difference you hope to achieve with your speaking.

I will encourage you to push yourself and follow that burning desire in your heart to tell your story and share your message. But I don't believe in bullshitting you either.

Speaking is hard work and what I'm going to share with you in this book is going to be hard work. The only way to become the speaker you wish to become, is by putting in the work. You need to have the drive to put in that work.

If you have that drive, then let's continue.

I'd like to make a distinction here.

Having that drive doesn't mean you don't doubt yourself, feel inadequate or wonder what the hell you are doing.

In fact, you probably have that drive because you feel that way.

What is fascinating about all the great leaders we look up to and admire — Abraham Lincoln, Martin Luther King, Nelson Mandela — is that they had almost crippling self doubt.

They doubted their abilities and worthiness to be in the position they were in.

It is that humanity that made them the great leaders they were.

The narcissists never become the leaders we look up to and admire. They might obtain a title of leadership (CEO, General, President) but they rarely do anything meaningful.

Their misplaced confidence in their abilities means they don't try to improve.

As a result, they are unlikely to develop the skills required to make a great impact on others.

They might lack the doubt, but they also lack the drive.

Abraham Lincoln may have battled deep bouts of depression but do you doubt that he was driven to end slavery?

He was willing to put the existence of his country on the line to do what he believed to be right.

Nelson Mandela may not have wanted the limelight of leadership, yet do you doubt he was driven to end Apartheid in South Africa?

He was willing to spend 27 years in prison for the cause he believed in.

That is the difference between doubt and drive.

You can be filled with doubt yet still driven to succeed.

If you don't have that drive, you're going to struggle to make much impact as a speaker.

Doubt, on the other hand, we can work with. That is what this chapter is going to help you do — overcome this self-doubt.

Confidence-Competence Loop

Everything we outline in this chapter is going to be based on a key psychological principle: the Confidence-Competence loop. This process describes how we can get better at anything.

Let's put you in the driving seat… literally.

If you have a driving licence, you'll remember your driving lessons and driving test.

Think back to your first three lessons.

You didn't have a clue what you were doing did you?

The gears, the mirrors, the indicator. It was all a lot to take in, wasn't it?

Still, by the time you got to your fifth lesson, you were a little better at driving, weren't you?

As you do something more, you get a little better at it.

This is the 'competence' part of the loop.

What can you remember after those first set of lessons?

Were you quite as nervous about getting in the car in subsequent lessons as you were the first time?

Were you quite as frazzled trying to remember all the different protocols you needed to follow?

I'm guessing not quite so much, correct?

You were a little more confident about getting behind the wheel.

Why?

Because you knew the basics.

You didn't have to think about how to change the gears, it had become automatic.

You didn't have to think about indicating when turning, it had become automatic.

You didn't have to think about checking your mirrors, it had become automatic.

Your improving skill as a driver had made you a little more confident.

That's the 'confidence' part of the loop.

What happens next?

That improved confidence meant that you were now ready to negotiate junctions, roundabouts and handle parking.

Feeling more confident means you are now ready to try harder things.

As you try more complex manoeuvres, you become a better driver and further increase your competence.

That's how the Confidence-Competence loop feeds itself.

It's the same with speaking.

You don't start confident. No-one does.

You have to stutter and stumble and sweat your way through as you begin your speaking journey.

You don't know what to do with your hands. You don't know where to look. You're desperately concentrating to try and remember the next word to come out of your mouth.

Nobody sits in a car and knows how to drive on their first lesson. No-one stands on stage for the first time and knows how to be an engaging speaker.

You have to activate the Confidence-Competence loop.

How do you do that?

You need to do more speaking.

I'm sure you'd love a sexy hack or shortcut to being a confident speaker.

There isn't one though.

You simply have to embrace the struggle and honour the process.

As you speak more, you will get better at it. As you get better at it, you will be more confident at it.

Whilst we are going to cover certain principles and practices in the rest of the chapter that is going to help this process, remember they are not substitutes for repeatedly putting yourself on the stage.

Create Your Speaker Identity

I believe that to become anything in life, speaker or otherwise, you need to ingrain that desire within you, as an identity.

Usain Bolt doesn't 'do' sprinting, he is an athlete.

Beyonce doesn't 'do' singing, she is an entertainer.

Stephen King doesn't 'do' writing, he is an author.

You don't want to 'do' speaking, you are a speaker. This isn't something you are thinking about. You have made the decision already because you are reading this book.

I believe that the most successful speakers have seen the stage as a destiny for themselves, something that they were 'just meant to do'. It's why Martin Luther King became a reverend and Nelson Mandela became a lawyer. They knew that they were supposed to stand and address audiences.

I want you to start describing yourself as a speaker, long before you are one.

When I returned from Experts Academy, I had decided that I was going to be a speaker. Of course the challenge was, that I hadn't actually spoken anywhere!

I wasn't going to let that stop me though. I dressed in my smartest clothes and my future wife and myself went to our old university. I snuck into one of the empty lecture theatres and started pretending to speak to the empty chairs. My future wife sat in the audience and took a few photos of me. To the camera it looked like I was delivering a lecture to an audience of students.

I created a tab on my website labelled 'Speaking' and uploaded the photo. There I was: 'Speaker for Hire'.

I started attending networking groups and when asked what I did, I would say 'Speaker'.

I made a promotional video for my speaking services. Naturally it was terrible because I had no idea what I was speaking about or who I was looking to serve as a speaker.

I started to call up companies, schools, and organisations telling them I was a speaker and offering my services.

Being a speaker was a belief for me. It didn't matter that I wasn't actually speaking. I had decided that I was a speaker and I was going to make it happen.

I don't believe in positive affirmations. I didn't stand in front of the mirror telling myself: "I am an amazing speaker" and "I am going to inspire millions of people from the stage". This is not about developing an empty, short-term 'feel-good' factor. This is about establishing a long-term identity.

When you plant the seed of speaking into your identity, it starts to change the decisions you make, the actions you take, and the outcomes you create.

When you say; "I am a Speaker" you are more likely to put yourself forward and pursue speaking opportunities.

When you say "I am a Speaker" organisers are more likely to hire you as a speaker.

When you say "I am a Speaker", your audience are more likely to believe what you say when you are on stage.

Your identity creates your actions and your actions dictate your outcomes, so choose your identity wisely.

Archive Positive Feedback

I'll be honest with you. This process of creating your speaker identity can be a tricky one. It can feel a little delusional in the dark times when no-one is watching your videos, no-one is hiring you to speak and no-one is signing up for your events.

That's why I think it's helpful to have some external reminders from time to time.

Even at the start of your speaking journey, you are going to find people who believe in you.

When I started calling anyone I thought would give me a stage, the Glasgow Association of Mental Health gave me a chance: my first ever gig.

When I ran my first ever workshop, I only had to twist the arms of half the audience to come along and support me. The other half actually bought tickets.

When I ran my first full-day event, three of the attendees gave me video testimonials.

In my first year as a speaker I had four separate people who mentored me and supported me, all for free, because they saw something in me that I did not fully see in myself at the time.

It is important to acknowledge and savour these external sources of validation when they arise.

It's very easy to get stuck in what's going wrong and what you aren't able to do in your speaking journey and miss these signs of support and encouragement.

That's why I recommend building an archive of any positive feedback you get.

If someone leaves a nice comment on one of your videos, screenshot it.

If someone sends you a grateful email, put that in a special folder.

If someone gives you a glowing review, print it out and stick it up somewhere that you can see it.

These pieces of positive feedback add up over time and they start to support the image you have of yourself as a speaker.

Standing in an empty lecture theatre pretending to speak to an audience doesn't make you feel much like a speaker, I'm not going to lie.

People thanking you for your talk and saying you're a great speaker does though.

These pieces of external feedback then combine with your internal work to solidify your speaking identity.

You film a video because that's what speakers do AND someone leaves a nice comment on it.

You secure a speaking gig after putting yourself out there continuously AND the organiser gives you a fantastic testimonial afterwards.

You work your butt off to create, market and run an event AND one of your students asks to record a praise-filled video to share how much they've taken from it.

You've done the inner work and seen the external reward.

When you keep an archive of all the times you have seen these external rewards, you start to recognise that your efforts are not in vain. They are helping you to become the speaker you know you can be.

During the difficult times when you are losing faith in the speaking journey, you can draw upon this extensive archive and reinforce the fact that you are doing a good job and you are going in the right direction as a speaker.

Inspiration Not Comparison

A lot of speakers, both beginners and advanced, walk a tightrope. It is the tightrope of admiration.

I hear many speakers say that they have been inspired by someone like Tony Robbins or Oprah Winfrey to become a speaker.

Who do you think was your inspiration to become a speaker? Who is the speaker you look up to most?

It's great to have a role model and someone to look up to but you need to be careful.

The tightrope you walk is trying to stay balanced on inspiration and not fall to the lethal depths of comparison.

When you look up to someone, it is very easy to compare yourself to this person.

You start comparing your social media followers, audience sizes and income.

You start thinking: *"They have X but I only have Y"*.

Rather than being encouraged, you are really getting discouraged.

Because you aren't where they are, you feel like giving up. Or that what you're doing isn't worth the effort. Or, that you aren't making a difference to people's lives.

It's an easy trap to fall into. I've done it many times myself.

My role model, Brendon Burchard, has over five million followers on Facebook alone, has spoken to 30,000 people in a stadium and sells thousands of tickets to his events every year at $2,000 a ticket.

Those are some pretty intimidating numbers to look up to.

Therefore, you need to monitor your internal dialogue when you are following your role models.

Are you saying to yourself: *"If they can do it, I can do it too."*

Or are you saying to yourself: *"They've done it so why haven't I?"*

See the difference?

Your role models are there to show you what's possible, not to use as a measuring stick for your success.

I get excited at the thought that I could speak to a stadium of people, but I don't beat myself up because I'm not doing it right now.

Their journey is not your journey. You have to focus on what the next step is for you. Keep your eyes on that tightrope. If you don't, you're going to fall into the pit of self-chastisement.

You can't make your unique contribution as a speaker if you are busy comparing yourself to someone else.

Them Not You

You walk onto stage. You see the expectant eyes looking back at you. You open your mouth to speak.

What are you thinking?

"What do I say next? Will they like me? Am I going to mess this up?"

Recognise this self talk?

This is self-centred thinking and you will never have your best impact as a speaker from this place.

The reason why people feel awkward and nervous on stage is because they are too focused on themselves.

They are thinking survival.

That's why public speaking is such a common fear, because people feel judged and threatened on stage as a result of this self-orientated thinking.

This isn't to say that you are selfish if you are thinking this way, it's just that your thinking is focused in the wrong place.

Everything shifts as a speaker when you realise it is about them, not about you.

Your inadequacies are not as important as the challenges you can help your audience solve.

If you are still worrying about what's going on for you then you don't have the energy to serve your audience.

This is what the great leaders we mentioned earlier realised. That is how Abraham Lincoln, Martin Luther King and Nelson Mandela rose above their fears and pain to create the change they desired. They knew that their message to others was more important than their own struggle.

When you turn the attention from you to them, you find you rise above your challenges. Fear dissipates. Tiredness subsides. Pain settles.

This is the place of leadership, where you can take on more and do more.

All through changing your focus.

As you prepare your speeches and you start feeling tired think to yourself *"this speech could change someone's life"* and you will find that extra spurt of energy to continue.

As you walk onto stage think *"How do I need to show up for this audience today"* and your nerves will relax.

When you finish your speech think *"I served to the best of my abilities today"* and the self-critical mind will quiet down.

As I said earlier, being a speaker is not a rockstar lifestyle. It is not about inflating your ego and sense of self-importance. It is about stepping into the responsibility of leadership and serving to the best of your abilities.

When you shift the focus from you to your audience, that is when you will discover the true scale of your speaking abilities.

<u>Four Year Vision</u>

One of my greatest challenges during my journey has been impatience. My desire to be further ahead and to be doing more with my work. This is an opponent that you will probably find yourself confronting too.

"Why are my audiences still only in single figures?"

"Why can't I get a paid speaking gig?"

"Why can't I sell my products and programs to people?"

There will be times when you feel frustration at your current circumstances, and a feeling that you should be further ahead than where you are now.

During these times, it is important to get perspective on how far you've travelled up until that point, and focus on the long-term vision of where you are going.

A perspective shift I have found helpful is to think back to my time at university.

It takes at least four years to get a degree. (I ended up taking five years). There is no 'hack' or 'accelerator' for getting a degree. It is the same four year program for everyone. Each semester you attend the classes, complete the assignments and pass the exams. If you do this semester after semester, year after year, you will get a degree at the end.

You have to honour that four year process. Over those four years, you will change and grow as a person. They are not four years of equal growth and development. Each year you can observe yourself at a different level of growth. You will see this in university, and you will see it in your speaking too. I name each of these years.

Clueless First Year

For many students, university is the first time they have left home. They have moved city, or even moved country. They are still finding themselves. They are learning the basics of organising and sustaining themselves. They are trying to integrate into new social circles. They are learning about a subject at a deeper level than they have previously, or they are learning about an entirely new subject. Almost every day is a learning experience in some manner for them.

This will be the same for you when you are speaking. You will still be trying to define who you are as a speaker and what your speaking style is. You will be trying to organise talks, keep to time and remember your points. You will be still learning how to film good video (or even film at all!). You will be learning about how to create and market a compelling event. You will be stumbling along throughout this first year, but that's okay. Clueless First Year doesn't last forever.

Curious Second Year

By the time you get to second year of university, you've managed to put down some roots. You've learned the basics of managing and surviving on your own. You've established some relationships and membership of certain groups. You've picked up the basics of your subject matter. If you're lucky, you've even learned a couple of things about yourself too.

What happens now is that you start to expand. You start looking at different places to hang out. You start meeting new people. You start to become interested in certain parts of your study over others. You try new things and take on new challenges. You become curious about what you are going to do next.

This is the first shift you will experience in your speaking too. After a time you will develop a certain level of proficiency in your speaking. You are more comfortable on stage and camera. You are starting to speak to bigger audiences. You can start to deliver a speech more from the heart and less from rehearsal. When you market an event people are getting more excited about it than they did before: you don't have to badger friends and acquaintances to drag them into the room to boost your numbers.

From this point, you are starting to think what you can do next. What new content could you teach or how could you enhance and develop what you are already teaching? Could you try delivering a talk or workshop in a new location? Could you make a product or program to expand upon what you are talking about?

Competent Third Year

By third year of university, you are starting to feel comfortable. You know where you are, who you hang out with and what you're doing. You have developed your skill in your subject matter. You have made more decisions about what you are going to study and you now understand what is required for the research and coursework. You are starting to resemble a functioning adult and worker.

One day, you will find yourself resembling a functioning speaker. You will think *"Wow, that talk went really well"* or *"Hey, I'm starting to speak far more often now"*. This reflects your shift into competence as per the Confidence-Competence loop. You are genuinely a good speaker now. You can deliver a speech flawlessly. You can speak to larger audiences. You can market yourself effectively. You're even starting to make decent money from this speaking malarky. You are starting to 'get' speaking.

At this point, you are doing well, but you aren't quite where you want to be. A third year student is doing okay but is ultimately working towards that degree. As a third year speaker you are doing okay but there is still something larger you are aiming towards. You aren't yet where you want to be. That only starts to click in your fourth and final year.

Confident Fourth Year

In their last year of university, students know what they need to do and how to do it. They organise and schedule their life as if on autopilot. They stick with the same band of companions. They know how to motivate themselves and be productive. They know what they're interested in and passionate about and they focus on that as much as possible. They know what they need to do to succeed and get to where they want to go. Their eye is now very much on the prize.

This will be the final shift in your speaking. You will gain a deep clarity on what you're doing. You will be able to step into a space where speaking is effortless and fluid. You will find your audiences growing organically. You will begin to notice the difference in your impact on others and the impact on your bank account.

This is not to say that you will be coasting and not having to try. This transition is still built on a ton of effort. Students work more in their last year than in any other year. You will find this too. However, the outcome of all that effort will be that much greater than when you started. In your first year, you had to work your butt off to deliver a one-hour speech to half a dozen people. In your fourth year, you will be working your butt off to deliver an eight-hour workshop to dozens of people.

I want you to see your speaking career as a four-year journey, just as you would going to university. It's not magically going to happen overnight. You are only going to notice the differences year on year, rather than week on week.

Here's the other thing to remember about university. Four years isn't the finished article. People haven't finished when they graduate, they are just beginning. That four-year process has been necessary just to prepare them for the real deal. It will take four years just to prepare you for the real deal.

I want you to think about this four-year vision, and what you want to build in these four years. When I began my speaking career, right there in Experts Academy, I knew exactly what I wanted to build towards: running my own multi-day event. That was my four-year vision. Four years after the death of my dad, in July 2019, I ran my first ever multi-day event. I had built the skill and confidence over those four years to pull it off. I had completed my studies. Now my career as a speaker was truly about to begin.

What is going to be your graduation? What are you building towards and, most importantly, why are you building towards it?

Maybe you want to deliver a TEDx talk. Maybe you want to be invited to speak in a different country. Maybe you want to be paid a four-figure or even five-figure sum for your speaking. Have an idea of what your 'graduation' is going to be, and spend four years studying how to make it happen.

<u>Build Your Mindset</u>

The journey of a speaker is a tough one. You will doubt yourself and your abilities. You will get tough gigs and you will run events that don't go well. You will be ignored and you will be criticised.

If you can keep your mind in the right place, you can push through these challenges. In this chapter we have explored different ways you can do this.

You learned about the Confidence-Competence loop and how the only path to true confidence as a speaker is simply to do more speaking.

You learned how to create your speaker identity and see yourself as a speaker before you even become one.

You learned the importance of archiving positive feedback so that you can see the external results of your internal efforts.

You learned the difference between inspiration and comparison so that you can stay focused on your journey and not get demotivated by what other people are doing.

You learned the important switch from you to them, so that you can step into the place of service and leadership and rise above your own challenges.

You learned how to prepare for a four-year journey as a speaker so that you know how to navigate the different stages of your speaking journey.

Once your mind is in the right place, you'll be able to push on as a speaker and get your voice heard. What is that voice going to say? That is what we are going to explore in the next chapter, where you are going to learn how to find your Message.

Chapter 5: Message

"Our challenge now is to make the very best of us, a daily reality."

"Because we are not immune to the viruses of hate, of fear, of other. We never have been. But we can be the nation that discovers the cure."

"And so to each of us as we go from here, we have work to do, but do not leave the job of combatting hate to the government alone. We each hold the power, in our words and in our actions, in our daily acts of kindness. Let that be the legacy of the 15th of March. To be the nation we believe ourselves to be."

(Jacinda Ardern. Christchurch Memorial Speech, 2019.)

Off the south of mainland Japan lie the islands of Okinawa.

These islands have stunning natural beauty but there is something even more remarkable about them.

This is where you find the world's longest-living people.

The average life expectancy is well into the 80s and the islands boast a higher percentage of centenarians (100+) and supercentenarians (110+) than anywhere else in the world.

Why do the people here live so long?

Several lifestyle factors have been identified but there is something deeper behind their longevity.

The Japanese call it 'Ikigai'.

Ikigai translates broadly as 'life worth living' but more specifically as 'The happiness of always working'.

Ikigai is your 'why' for living and the Okinawans have a deep connection with their Ikigai.

They seem to live for longer because they understand why they are alive. Whether that be catching fish to feed their family; practicing medicine to heal the sick or composing music to entertain the community; they see their role in the world and live it day-to-day.

In their culture, there is no word for 'retirement' because they don't understand why you would retire from your life's purpose.

I think as speakers we can learn a lot from this concept of Ikigai.

Our message is what we live for as speakers. It is something we stand for every day. It is not a message we 'retire' from or cast aside. It is something we live and breathe and that is where our purpose in life comes from.

Getting clarity on that message ignites the fire in your belly as a speaker. It gives you the energy to work on your craft day after day and the power to inspire those you speak to.

Like a lot of speakers, I'm sure you started with that initial drive to speak, but don't necessarily have the clarity on what you are specifically going to speak about.

That is what you are going to learn in this chapter.

We are going to nail down your message and find your speaking Ikigai.

Gain From Pain

The first place I encourage you to go is to think of your personal story and struggle. That after all is why you are going down this path, right? You didn't look at a university prospectus or a job site and see 'public speaker' listed there and decide to give it a go.

I believe being a speaker is not something you fall into, it is something that destiny pulls you towards. What was your particular destiny?

Did you have a health scare? Did you go bankrupt? Did you suffer a broken heart? What was it that drove you to want to inspire others?

This is a story that you have to connect with and share if you are going to inspire others. People don't care about your title or your credentials, they care about your story.

So you're a personal trainer.

So you're an internet marketer.

So you're a relationship coach.

In the words of Shania Twain, that don't impress me much.

Trainers, marketers, and coaches are a dime a dozen. Why should I care about you any more than the other wannabes out there?

I'll care because of the story you tell me.

You're a personal trainer because you struggled with depression.

You're an internet marketer because you were a single mum raising three children.

You're a relationship coach because you were left at the altar.

Now I feel different about you. Now I understand your motivation and can connect with you so much deeper than your compatriots.

We as humans create meaning through stories. We will talk about the power of stories to create meaning and connection with your audience later. But a speaker's first audience member is always themselves.

You connect with your message when you connect with your personal story. When you understand why you are delivering a workshop in the pub basement; why you are facing your fears by stepping to the front of a room of strangers; why you spend entire evenings practicing a speech when everyone is out having fun; that is what gives you the motivation to do it time after time.

I want you to return to that personal story again and again. You'll refer to it on stage, but also have that as a consistent narrative in all the behind-the-scenes work you have to do.

When you doubt yourself, get nervous, or feel tired, I want you to remember this personal story. I want you to remember that 'why'. Pain can be an incredible motivator in our lives. If you have a story of pain and struggle (and we all do in some way) use that to drive you on to greater things. Use that to push you beyond your boundaries and create a better life for you and the people you serve.

Two Magic Questions

Every business, speaking or otherwise, must know the answer to two critical questions.

1) What problem do I solve?
2) Who do I solve it for?

If you have good answers to these questions, then you have a good business. I remember when I first started, my answers were rubbish.

The problem that I solved was 'any'.

The people that I served was 'anyone'.

When you try to be everything to everyone, you end up being nothing to no one.

So I found myself struggling to get heard because I didn't make it clear who I was and what I did.

I came across these questions relatively soon on my business journey but I struggled to answer them.

My problem was that the questions are so broad, that they make you think of broad answers. I needed a specific question to give me a specific answer. I've managed to find those questions, with a little help.

One day I was brainstorming with one of my mentors and we were trying to answer the second of these questions 'Who do I solve it for?'. I was drawing these mind-maps and writing all kinds of demographic information on them 'Female', '30-50', 'Married', 'Children', 'Liberal' and not getting anywhere. I felt I was just making it up as I went along and didn't have a sense of what type of person I was trying to describe.

My mentor could see my confusion, so asked me a simple but powerful question. "David, who do you want to be a hero to?"

That question changed the game for me because instead of this faceless amalgamation of demographic information, I saw a real person.

Who I wanted to be a hero to… was me.

Specifically, it was me at eighteen years old. I was someone who was intelligent but tended to hide it and play dumb. I was someone who had a dream but was too scared to pursue and commit to it. I was someone who was warm and caring but lacked the confidence to show it. I knew I could do better. I had the ability to start writing and speaking at the age of eighteen, but I didn't have the belief in myself to Rise and Inspire. I was someone with a lot to offer who needed to get out of his own goddamn way and step up.

That was who I wanted to help: who I was at eighteen. It didn't mean I wanted to help eighteen-year-old men. It meant I wanted to help people who were getting in the way of their ability. I wanted to help people who had far more to offer the world than what they were currently doing (sound like you?).

I wanted to help people in this situation. That could be eighteen-year-old students, twenty-eight-year-old professionals, thirty-eight-year-old divorcees or forty-eight-year-old empty-nesters. The demographics didn't matter. It was the person behind the demographics and what they were experiencing. My mentor's question allowed me to unlock this.

My mentor re-conceptualised one of these key questions and helped me find the answer. I knew who I wanted to serve and I started to get an idea of why I wanted to serve them. What I needed to do now was get more clarity on what problem I solved.

I think we also need to reframe the first question, just as my mentor helped me reframe the second question. I have thought of a couple of different variations of this question, but the one I like best is: 'What problem is unacceptable to you?'

Let's face it, there's plenty of things we would like to get rid of in the world: hunger, poverty, disease, war, etc. There's also plenty of problems you have the skill to solve: admin, sales, planning, repair, whatever your particular training and experience has given you the ability to do.

However, what is one problem that really irks you? What is something that you say to yourself *"how has no one done anything about that yet?"* or *"why aren't people doing more to address this issue?"*.

Do you see people who are obese and ask: *"why are we not looking after ourselves properly?"*. Do you see teenagers with scars on their wrists and ask: *"why are we not supporting our young ones more?"* Do you look around a coffee shop and see tables of people sitting on their phones and ask: *"why are we losing connection with each other?"*

This perspective is a clue to a problem you are passionate about and motivated to solve. This problem then feeds into the way you speak and the topics you speak about.

When I started to investigate the answer to this question for myself, I realised the problem that was unacceptable to me was lack of education.

At eighteen years old, I could be considered a success of the education system. I had gone to a high-performing school where the question was not "are you going to university?" it was "which university are you going to?". I had earned good grades that ensured that the university I was going to was a Russell Group university with one of the top five psychology departments in the UK.

Education is about more than academics though. At eighteen I was on the verge of years of mental health issues, I was not pursuing my true dream to be an author and I couldn't hold down a long-term relationship. Yes, I might be good at writing essays and passing exams, but I did not have a clue about happiness, purpose, or love.

I see a big gap in our education system; that it builds knowledge, not character. It doesn't do what I think should be its job: cultivating children's strengths and igniting their enthusiasm for what they do. The reason why you are reading this book is because school did not teach you nearly enough about public speaking, did it? The woeful education we get at school and in our workplaces turn us into boring PowerPoint robots, not speakers.

That is what I wanted to address in my work. I wanted to give people the education they don't receive at school. I wanted to educate people like eighteen-year-old David who hadn't been educated about the important things in life.

These two questions drive my speaking, and they will drive yours too. I would like you to think about these two questions now, and consider what your answers are.

1) What problem do you think is unacceptable?
2) Who do you want to be a hero to?

You should always be developing and deepening your answer to these two questions. As you progress on your journey, you will get greater clarity on these answers. These two answers drive everything you do. When you are engaging with your audience; planning events; creating curriculum and content; these two answers inform it all.

You Have A Dream

One of the greatest examples of inspiring speaking was Dr. Martin Luther King Jr.'s 'I Have a Dream' speech. 'I Have a Dream' was the last six-minute segment of a seventeen-minute speech delivered from the steps of the Lincoln Memorial in Washington D.C. on the 28th of August 1963.

Not nearly as many people are aware of the first eleven minutes of Dr. King's speech as they are those last six. What I find fascinating about this speech is that it was only supposed to last eleven minutes. King had only written a script for those first eleven minutes.

As he reached the end of those eleven minutes, a person in his entourage, gospel singer Mahalia Jackson, shouted: "Tell 'em about the dream Martin."

King had spoken of the dream on much smaller stages, but he had never planned to share it in front of the 250,000 amassed before him on the Washington Mall, the many thousands more watching on television, and the millions of people who would watch the recording in the future.

What makes the six minutes of 'I Have a Dream' so impressive was not just the content, but the fact that it was delivered off the cuff. At eleven minutes, King stopped speaking from the head and started speaking from the heart. I believe that this is where our power as speakers comes from.

You can tap into the power of this expression with what I call the 'You Have a Dream' exercise.

I'd like you to imagine that just like Martin Luther King, you are standing in Washington D.C. The crowd stretches out of sight, thousands of TV cameras are trained on you, broadcasting to every part of the world, translating into every language spoken by humans. Your audience is the entire population of the Earth. Every living person is listening to you and the message you are about to deliver.

You have six minutes to tell them something, those same six minutes that King used so effectively. What would you say?

As well as thinking about what you want to say in six minutes, I challenge you to write your speech in just six minutes. When we take too long to think about something and plan it out, we get stuck in our heads. Your power as a speaker comes from speaking from the heart.

With a six-minute time limit, you have no time to plan and strategise. You have to work on intuition and instinct. You automatically drop into your heart and express from there.

Give yourself these six minutes and find out what is in your heart. At my seminars, I encourage people to read out their dreams. I have not yet heard someone read out something that wasn't impactful, meaningful, and poetic. I'm sure yours will be no different.

What is contained in this six-minute speech is the message in your heart. It is part of what drives you and what you think the world should know. There are clues and hints in this speech as to how you should be speaking to your audiences and what you should be speaking to them about.

If you find you are focusing on telling people to travel, have fun, and do what they enjoy, perhaps you are meant to speak to people about happiness.

If you find you are focusing on telling people to do their best and chase their dreams, perhaps you are meant to speak to people about purpose.

If you find you are focusing on telling people to think about and help others, perhaps you are meant to speak to people about relationships.

You can use the 'You Have a Dream' speech to inform your work. You can even use portions of it during the talks you deliver.

When we are at our best as speakers is when we are speaking from the heart, and this exercise will help you to do that.

Embrace Your Style

The beauty of speaking is that it allows for individual expression. Whilst there are common principles of 'good speaking', there is also huge scope beyond this for being your own brand of speaker.

To start to find out what type of speaker you are. I have created a little quiz. This quiz has absolutely no scientific basis, like many of the 'what marvel superhero are you?' quizzes you'll see on Facebook, but it's a bit of fun that will help us introduce this section. Keep a track of your answers in the white space next to the question or on a notepad or your phone.

1) Which adjective best describes you?

A) Wise
B) Caring
C) Strong
D) Entertaining

2) In everyday conversation, what are you most likely to find yourself doing?

A) Asking questions
B) Offering advice
C) Giving instructions
D) Telling jokes

3) What type of films and television shows do you most enjoy watching?

A) Historical
B) Romance
C) Action
D) Comedy

4) What animal do you most associate with?

A) Owl
B) Dog
C) Lion
D) Monkey

5) What would you most like to change in others?

A) How they think
B) How they relate
C) How they act
D) How they feel

6) Which historical figure do you connect with most?

A) Nelson Mandela
B) Princess Diana
C) Emmeline Pankhurst
D) Charlie Chaplin

7) What type of work have you found yourself in through-out your career?

A) Creative
B) Team Projects
C) Practical
D) Customer-facing

8) What type of exercise are you most likely to do?

A) Yoga
B) Group Class
C) Weight-lifting
D) Dancing

9) How do you talk in normal conversation?

A) Calm and measured
B) Warm and soothing
C) Loud and direct
D) Silly and playful

10) On a quiet Saturday, with no obligations or responsib-ilities, what are you most likely to find yourself doing?

A) Reading a book
B) Meeting up with a friend
C) Building something
D) Playing a game

We'll come back to what your answers mean a little bit later.

Just now, I'd like you to think of Barack Obama, Oprah Winfrey, Mel Robbins, and Jerry Seinfeld. All of them are great speakers, but each we could say speak quite differently, don't they?

If you look at the most-watched TED talks, you will see a group of great speakers, but all with different styles of speaking. You will see Simon Sinek deliver with an insightful and poised manner in his talk 'Start with Why'; Brene Brown who delivers with heart and openness in her talk 'The Power of Vulnerability'; Tony Robbins who delivers with power and presence in his talk 'Why we do what we do' and the late Ken Robinson, who delivers great humour and witticisms in his talk 'Are Schools Killing our Creativity?'.

In your journey as a speaker, you are going to find a style that best suits you. There is no 'best style' for speaking. You can be equally impactful in different ways.

I have identified four main styles of speaking. All of us fit into one of these styles. We develop our preferred style and become exceptional at it. Simon Sinek is a fantastic speaker, but if you asked him to do stand-up comedy, he would probably struggle, because it's a very different style to what he has become proficient in.

To envision these four styles, I'd like you to picture a pack of cards. In a pack of cards, there are four types of face cards, and we can view the speaking styles through these cards.

The first face card is the King. The King is wise. He instructs and educates those he serves. The King speaks in a calm, articulate manner. His voice stays fairly level. His movements and gestures are slower and more thoughtful.

The second face card is the Queen. The Queen is adored. She supports and understands those she serves. The Queen speaks in a warm, comforting manner. Her voice drops a little lower. Her movements and gestures are open and inviting.

The third face card is the Jack. The Jack is strong. He fights for and champions those he serves. He speaks in an authoritative, motivating manner. His voice is loud. His gestures are composed and powerful.

The fourth face card is the Joker. The Joker is entertaining. He enlivens and energises those he serves. He speaks in a jovial, playful manner. His voice is fast and exciting. His gestures are flamboyant and enthusiastic.

Already, through these descriptions, you may have found yourself resonating with one over the other. There is a style that is more obvious to you as your style. If you would like to confirm this further, go back and look at your answers to the quiz.

If you mainly answered "A" for the questions, you are the **King**.

If you mainly answered "B" for the questions, you are the **Queen**.

If you mainly answered "C" for the questions, you are the **Jack**.

If you mainly answered "D" for the questions, you are the **Joker**.

If you are not entirely sure, go and watch those four TED speakers I described earlier. I picked them specifically because they are an archetype of each type of speaker. Simon Sinek is the King. Brene Brown is the Queen. Tony Robbins is the Jack. Ken Robinson is the Joker.

As you start speaking, you will begin to fall into an archetype quite quickly. For me, it was the King. I found comfort in speaking in a composed, thoughtful manner. To bring deep ideas and thoughtful discourse into my speaking. I found comfort in the controlled, thoughtful style of the King.

From your style, you can build the structure of your speeches and workshops. I knew that my strengths were well-articulated ideas and reflective exercises because that matches my energy and style. My seminars are still built around this backbone.

As you start to notice your style, you can build your speeches the same way. If you are the Queen, you may want to incorporate a lot of group activities into your speeches. If you are the Jack, you may want to bring a lot of energy and movement into your speeches. If you are the Joker, you may want to bring a lot of stories and anecdotes into your speeches.

As you start to build your preferred style, you will notice that it's not enough. No one is 100% one style. Additionally speaking in one style is boring for your audience. Think of it like films. Watching Tom Hanks films is great, but it can get a bit intense and lose its power if you just watch all these thoughtful films consecutively. Watching daft Will Ferrell films is fun, but it gets a bit banal and boring if you watch these funny films consecutively. Sometimes you are in the mood for a deep, moving film, other times you just want something cheap and cheerful.

As you become more experienced, you will start to notice the emergence of all styles. Whilst you will still retain a primary style the majority of the time, you will be able to flow into different styles. My King style allows me to bring insight and realisations to my audiences, but I need to be able to step into my Jack to make them act upon these ideas. I also need to step into my Joker Style to show them the joy and fun that comes from making these changes. I need to step into my Queen Style to help support them in making their changes.

Recognise that your power as a speaker is twofold. It comes from developing mastery in one particular style, and being known for that style. However, it also comes from having the flexibility to move into different styles to maximise your connection with and impact on the audience.

Find Your Message

Speaking is now a part of your purpose. You've felt that and that's why you've picked up this book. Your purpose involves sharing a unique message with the world, even if you don't know it yet.

In this chapter, we have looked to steer you in the right direction to clarify what your message is.

You learned how to draw upon your story of pain to bring meaning to your message.

You learned how to answer the two important questions that help you home in on your message.

You learned how to use the 'You Have a Dream' exercise to uncover the messages within you that you might not be aware of.

You learned how to find your speaking style so you can play to your strengths and speak in a way that feels natural to you.

When you start to get clearer on your message, you next want to learn how to articulate it well. How do you become the engaging speaker who can get that message heard by the people who need to hear it? In the next chapter you are going to learn how to develop that required Mastery.

Chapter 6: Mastery

"I done wrassled with an alligator. I done tussled with a whale. I done handcuffed lightnin', throwed thunder in jail! That's bad…"

"Only last week I murdered a rock; injured a stone; hospitalized a brick. I'm so mean I make medicine sick!"

"Bad! Fast… Fast! Last night I cut the light off in my bedroom, hit the switch, was in the bed before the room was dark! "

"Fast! And you, George Foreman — all of you chumps are gonna bow, when I whoop him. All of ya! I know you got him, I know you got him

picked... but the man's in trouble. I'mma show you how great I am."

(Muhammed Ali. "Rumble in the Jungle" Press Conference, 1974.)

No one starts out good. In fact, no one starts out average.

When you begin your journey as a speaker, you are going to suck. That might not sound very motivational, but it actually is.

Because you should remember that everyone sucked when they were at the same stage you are.

It's comforting to know that Barack Obama sucked at one time, yet he can appear as Mr. Cool now.

If they can progress from suck to spectacular, why can't you? There's only one thing standing in your way.

Practice.

The more you speak, the better you get. There's no way around it.

Furthermore, it's not just the speaking you do on stage that counts. It's the work behind the scenes.

What you consider to be 'speaking', those moments on stage, are about 10% of what it means to be a speaker. If you watch someone's inspiring 60-minute keynote, you can bet they've spent at least ten hours making it good. If it is a seasoned pro, they have probably put a hundred hours of work into perfecting that 60-minute keynote.

This chapter is all about that process of mastery, the 90+% of what it means to be a speaker.

No hack or gimmick will make you a good speaker. There are, however, processes that will guide and support you and that's what we are going to explore in this chapter.

The Nine Principles of Mastery (9PM)

In my years teaching — first personal development and then public speaking — I was able to identify nine principles that built mastery. You need to hit most of them, if not all of them, to grow.

The mistake that most people make is that they focus on skill development in far too narrow a way. They think that just doing the thing automatically means they get better at it.

Whilst this is true, it is only a small part of the picture. Did you learn to read by just staring at a page again and again? Of course not. There were all sorts of steps and processes you undertook to develop the ability to read this book.

These nine principles are spread across three areas of learning. True mastery comes when you integrate these three areas.

We'll go through these three areas and break down the three principles that make each one up and how that applies to building mastery in speaking.

Practical

The first area is the most obvious. This is doing the thing that you are trying to build mastery in, whether that be painting, cooking, or public speaking.

Most people only think about this area, meaning they can only ever hit three of the principles. Sometimes they don't even get that far as they don't understand this area fully.

Let's break down what these first three principles are.

1) Identify: How do you develop your desired skill?

You might think this is easy. "I want to be better at speaking David" I hear you say.

Before you move on from this principle too quickly, let's pause.

What exactly do you need to do to become a better speaker?

Do you struggle to articulate your points? Going off on tangents and umming and erring through your speeches.

Do you struggle to express yourself on stage? Do you speak with your hand in your pockets, frozen to one spot on the stage with a pained grimace on your face?

Do you struggle to connect with your audience? Do they stare at you blankly, have to get answers syringed out of them when you ask a question, and — worst of all — not get any of your jokes?

You have to identify what you need to focus on to advance as a speaker.

This will change over time and the next eight principles adapt accordingly.

So, you are not just developing 'public speaking', you are developing a specific aspect of public speaking.

You have to be clear on what that is to be able to work through this process.

2) Stretch: Challenge yourself just beyond your current capabilities

I want you to imagine you have just started yoga (or remember when you did).

If you go into a yoga class and sit on the floor cross-legged for the entire session, you aren't going to get any more flexible.

Equally, if you try to yank your leg behind your head in your first class, you are going to injure yourself.

You need to find the sweet spot between challenging yourself and getting way out of your depth.

Remember the term: "stretch, not snap".

To return to speaking: you've identified what aspect of speaking you want to improve in the first principle.

Next, you need to find a challenge that is in the "stretch, not snap" sweet spot.

If you are someone who is currently using a lot of 'filler words' — um, er, ah, you know, so, like — then aiming for a speech that is word-perfect without any hesitations is probably a step too far.

Instead, you might say "I want to reduce my ums, ers, and ahhs by 50%" or "I want to complete a speech without using the phrase 'you know'".

When assessing this, the key point I want to make is that you still feel a little uncomfortable. Many people play too small when trying to improve.

Yes, you shouldn't get off your couch and try to run a marathon. At the same time, if you stop running as soon as you get out of breath, then you are never going to get up to that marathon.

Don't snap, but don't coast either.

3) Measure: Find a parameter of progress and record consistently

The management expert Peter Drucker said: "you can't manage what you don't measure".

If you don't measure what you are doing, you have no idea whether you are getting better.

Measurement is much easier with skills that have objective parameters: the fastest runner wins the race and the investor with the most profit is the richest.

Speaking may appear a little more challenging at first as there aren't obvious parameters to measure.

There are though.

When I started, I wanted to increase my speaking stamina. This was measured by how long I was on stage. I started with two-hour workshops, then graduated to eight-hour seminars, then moved to sixteen-hour summits.

My measurement metric was just time on stage and could I increase that?

There are all sorts of other metrics you can use:

- Number of videos published per month
- Number of 'filler words' used in a speech
- Number of times your hands were clasped in a 'defensive' posture
- How many speaking gigs you book per year
- Monthly income from speaking

The important thing is that you can identify the key metric that helps you determine your progress.

It's okay if the metric isn't moving, or is progressing slowly because that gives you feedback as to how effective your method for increasing it is.

I found this in my example of trying to increase my speaking stamina.

Trying to do it with big eight-hour events was actually too slow, as a lot of work had to go into creating and marketing them.

I found that running more frequent four-hour events was much easier to do and meant that I could get on stage a lot more frequently and speak in more locations to grow my audience faster.

That's the type of assessment and adjustment you can make when you have measurement criteria.

Psychological

The second area of mastery is psychological. Whatever skill you might be building, the learning for that is based in the brain. Public speaking is no different.

Especially given the emotional aspects of public speaking — stage nerves, storytelling, audience interaction — it's particularly important to have your mind in the right place when it comes to speaking.

You can have all of the technical skills of a good speaker, but not be able to create the impact you desire in the world. The skills are actually the easy bit.

I believe anyone can learn the 'skills' of speaking: voice, gestures, storytelling structures, etc. Learning the psychology of being a good, or hopefully great speaker, will be a very different matter.

That's what the next three principles of mastery focus on.

4) Meaning: Know your 'why': why this practice, and the results, are so important to you

This is arguably the single most important factor for me. If you plan the other eight principles of mastery, but you don't have this, I'm not putting money on you succeeding.

However, if all you have is a 'why', I'll back you to find a way. Everything else can be trained, but the 'why' has to come from you.

We've explored some elements of finding your 'why' in the previous chapter. I want you to reconnect with them and refocus on them during your speaking journey.

Never lose sight of why you wanted to become a speaker in the first place. During the difficult times of practicing speeches, scrambling for gigs, and speaking to disinterested audiences, it's easy to despair and even want to pack it all in.

The speaker with the strong enough 'why' will push through the process of mastery and become the speaker they are capable of being.

5) Aspire: Set high expectations for what you can do and achieve

I've grown up in Scotland, which is a wonderful country in so many ways. One thing it is not though is aspirational.

Our culture is one where we put ourselves down and accept our lot in life. We have this inferiority complex that creeps into everything that we do: sports, business, politics.

In 2018, Croatia, a country with 70% of the population of Scotland who was embroiled in regional war just a few decades ago, reached the final of the Football World Cup.

Scotland, who played the first-ever international football match, hasn't even qualified for the tournament since 1998.

That comparison for me pretty much sums up our mentality as a country.

We don't believe in ourselves and aspire for better.

When it comes to speaking, don't be like Scotland. Be like Croatia.

You have to believe that you are capable of feats beyond your current abilities.

Set yourself larger targets.

One of the common targets amongst speakers is to speak at TEDx.

I think this is a good target to have as part of your speaking journey, but it shouldn't be the end goal.

The fact is, if you apply to enough TEDx events, you'll always be able to find a smaller one that will let you in.

I've met several speakers who have done a TEDx who aren't very good speakers.

Having a TEDx talk isn't an aspirational goal for a speaker.

Having a 'real' TED talk though is a whole different story.

The type of speaker you need to be to secure a TEDx talk is very different from the type of speaker who gets invited to speak at *the* TED.

Absolutely have a TEDx talk (or multiple ones) as part of the journey, but set your sights high on getting to the top of TED.

That creates a whole different mentality for how you approach your speaking and your subject material.

To get a TEDx, you have to be good. Anyone can learn to be good.

To get a TED, you have to be unique. That is a far harder height to reach.

When you have aspirational thinking, it forces you to completely change how you approach your speaking. You need that different approach to get different results.

6) Visualise: Mentally rehearse excellence

Mental rehearsal across a variety of fields has been shown to improve performance.

One of the mistakes that I know people make when they are practicing is they recite a script from the page, or they stand and look at themselves in the mirror.

You need to animate your speaking much more than this. You need to imagine how you move on stage. You need to imagine how you look around the room. You need to imagine how you gesture towards and interact with the audience.

The images that you create in your head replicate themselves on stage.

Ever imagined that you would forget your lines... and you did.

Ever imagined that you would stumble over that particular word or sentence… and you did.

Ever imagined tripping on the stairs up to the stage… and you did.

You've seen it work against you, now see it work for you.

I used visualisation in my second national public speaking championship in 2019.

The previous year I had finished 2nd overall, which was a fantastic debut. Nonetheless, I actually finished ahead of the winner in the previous qualifying round, so I felt I had been capable of getting first place and fallen short.

This year, I wanted to go that one step further.

The venue for this year's contest was poor, it had been chosen for its budget rather than its functionality.

It was an auditorium in a church building and it had a massive pillar front and centre on the stage.

I had seen every previous speaker struggling with this pillar. It forced you to favour one side of the stage over the other; to get to the other side of the stage you had to quickly run behind it, or side shuffle in front of it. It broke your eye contact with parts of the audience. You could barely stand in front of it without spitting all over the front row of the audience.

I realised the secret to winning in this contest was to 'manage' the pillar better than everyone else.

All the other contestants had been avoiding this pillar, putting them on the defensive when they were speaking.

I went on the offensive. I looked at this pillar and visualised all the different things that I could do with it when it was my time to get on stage. I imagined performing these different actions and how they would fit into my speech. There were two actions that I could imagine in my mind having a positive effect on the quality of my speech.

When I found myself on stage, one of the first things I did was stand by the pillar, stretch my arm out, and touch it. "Every speaker today has been struggling with this pillar," I told the audience. I was the first speaker to not just acknowledge the elephant in the room, but stroke it too.

In my mental rehearsal of this moment, I had imagined myself standing confidently, legs apart and head raised, looking deep into the centre of the audience, showing that I was not afraid of this pillar like the other speakers had been. I was replicating that now.

The pillar made an appearance right at the start of the speech and it returned at the end. My final line was: "You can take your speaking…"

I attached myself to the pillar and swung around the back of it, popping out the opposite side and holding a pose like a pole dancer.

"…a full 180".

There were hoots of laughter from the audience and I held that pose as I had imagined again and again in my head. Still hanging from the pillar, I gestured to the contest chair and gave the stage back to him.

I sat down, pleased that those two moments had played out exactly how I had visualised them in my head.

I was awarded 1st place in that contest, my first national championship.

I still believe that the 2nd placed contestant had a better speech than I did. His content was deeper and more developed than mine was. What won it was my performance. It hadn't been what I said, it had been how I said it.

If I had grabbed that pillar at the end and slipped off, I know I wouldn't have won that contest. It would've been the last thing that the audience remembered, including the judges. I risked everything on that single move and it paid off.

It wasn't a risk though because I had already executed that move dozens of times in my head before I even took to stage. That is the power of mental rehearsal.

It is not enough to practice what you say as a speaker, you need to practice how you say it. You need to see yourself executing the desired action again and again in your mind and replicate it in reality.

There's a really important distinction to make here. You visualise the desired action, not the desired result.

I didn't sit there in the audience imagining myself receiving a standing ovation. I didn't imagine myself standing there with the 1st place trophy. That's woo-woo positive thinking that doesn't get you anywhere.

You need to visualise the process, not the result. You visualise the run, not the finish line. You think about how you engage in the process with excellence, and the result sorts itself out.

People

The part that people miss out of their mastery journey is socialising their learning.

There is a perception that mastery is a solitary activity: you have to hide in a cave and meditate, wake up early to go for a lonely run, or stay up late at night coding on a computer.

The reality is far different. Mastery does not exist in a bubble. Other people are one of the most important aspects of your development as a speaker.

This is the reason why I have been a member of Toastmasters for as long as I have. To be honest, I don't learn much from Toastmasters the organisation, such as its learning resources and structure, but I learn so much from the people who are in the organisation.

Three social principles play a huge role in your mastery. The previous six principles will make you good. These next three will make you great.

7) Coach: Find an expert who knows more than you do

Your coach is someone who knows how to train expertise in your area. This could be someone who is an expert themselves, for example, if you want to improve your tennis, I'm sure Roger Federer and Serena Williams could give you some pretty good advice.

However, often a coach isn't someone who is that much of an expert themselves, but they are fantastic at bringing out the expertise in others.

If you look at a football manager like Sir Alex Ferguson; he was a fairly average football player. But he cultivated the excellence in David Beckham, Wayne Rooney, Cristiano Ronaldo, and a whole host of other top football players.

If you look at rapper and producer Dr. Dre, he has achieved far more success as a producer than a rapper. He has launched the careers of Snoop Dogg, 50 Cent, Eminem, Kendrick Lamar, and loads of others in the Hip Hop industry.

I recommend two coaches. Firstly, a model of excellence at the top of your field to show you the possibilities.

Who is your speaking role model? Think back to the four speaker styles we talked about in the previous chapter. Who best typifies the style you want to emulate?

Absorb everything you can about that person. Not just videos of them speaking, but if there are any interviews with them, listen to those too. If they've written a book or had books written about them, read those too.

Getting the full insight into that role model demonstrates not just their results, but their journey too.

Did you know for example that Dr. Martin Luther King Jr. got 2 Cs for public speaking in school?

It's pretty interesting to find out how he went from that to 'I Have a Dream', right?

If you can find out how he made that journey, you can follow the process to improve your speaking too.

Secondly, who is a coach who can actively instruct you on how to reach those possibilities?

Who is someone who is in a position to watch you speaking and give you specific feedback on those speeches?

Family and friends aren't what we're looking for here, you need someone with insight into the techniques and fine arts of speaking.

This is one of the aspects I enjoy in Toastmasters; having other speakers who know what they're talking about giving me feedback and pointers on my speeches and speaking. That would be the first place I would point an aspiring speaker like yourself to find a coach if you are not a Toastmaster already.

8) Peers: Surround yourself with people who promote the skill you desire

Social conditioning is one of the defining forces of our life. If you show me the people you spend time with, it is possible to predict your life expectancy; salary; number of children; likelihood of addiction; voting preferences; relationship status; exercise habits; highest educational qualification and a whole host of other life factors. This is known as the 'social contagion' effect in scientific circles. We become like the people around us, so choose that company carefully.

You might not think that your relationships can affect your journey as a speaker, but they do.

Did your teachers at school encourage your participation or discourage it?

Do your friends want to hear your views or want to tell you theirs?

When you share an idea at a work meeting, is it valued or ignored?

How comfortable you are at speaking up and expressing yourself has already been determined by your relationships and life circumstances. The people you surround yourself with will continue to have that influence on you.

We want peers who promote the skills we desire. I define this in two different ways.

The first is to surround yourself with people who are working on the same skill you are.

Have you ever wondered why so many tech companies are based in Silicon Valley?

One of the big reasons is because it is a cluster of creative talent. It is a community of people on a similar wavelength, even if they are working for opposing companies.

If you want to be a speaker, then how many people do you know who are speakers? How often do you communicate with them and spend time with them?

When you are in the company of good speakers, what they do automatically rubs off on you. This is why I enjoy competing in speaking contests, as I get to be in the company of speakers of high quality. I pick up aspects of their demeanour and presentation that enhance what I do as a speaker, without being fully conscious of it. I integrate the idea of being a speaker into my identity, as we talked about in the mindset chapter because I am in the company of excellent speakers.

This is where I think the real 'secret' of Toastmasters lies. When you walk into a Toastmasters meeting, 100% of the attendees want to be better speakers. There are different skill levels in the room but you are all united in the same purpose. That is an energy that nourishes you in your journey as a speaker.

That is why we have the Rise and Inspire Speakers (RAIS) Facebook group; to share the journey with other speakers across the world. It can be difficult to find those like-minded peers along the journey.

The second is to hang around people who actively support your efforts.

One of the most difficult challenges you will face is trying to improve when the people around you don't support your efforts.

There are a host of subtle and not so subtle remarks that come your way when you're trying to do something different and positive.

They are the people who tell you that you're "too mouthy", "a little loud", " a bit intense" when you start finding your voice and expressing yourself.

These people do not have your best interests at heart when it comes to your speaking journey.

They find you "too mouthy" because they have little of value to say themselves.

They feel you are "a little loud" because they are afraid to speak up themselves.

They say you're "a bit intense" because they haven't found something they are passionate about.

Don't let their fears (which is what all of these comments are) bring you down. Find those who support your Rise.

There are people in your life who don't necessarily 'get' what you are doing or don't understand the intricacies of public speaking, but they will be encouraging nonetheless.

They might come to watch one of your speeches, share a video you post online, or even just ask how it's all going.

They aren't going to sit down and listen to draft after draft of a speech and give you feedback. But that's not their journey. They can support you on your speaking journey without being very actively involved in it.

Making sure that you have good people around you makes the world of difference.

9) Teach: Pass your knowledge on to someone else

As you develop a skill, you then become an expert to someone who knows less than you.

I'm going to let that sink in... because it opposes so many of the barriers I see beginner speakers make up.

"I haven't got enough experience to talk about this."

"Why would anyone listen to me?"

"I don't think I can help anyone"

"Even if I was a speaker, what would I talk about?"

You are an expert to ANYONE who knows less than you.

You don't have to have advanced very far at all to help someone along the journey.

Looking specifically at speaking, you may not have been speaking very long, but you might have learned a few things already.

You've learned how to go live on Facebook.

You've learned a trick to help you remember what you're going to say.

You've learned how to settle the nerves a little before you go on stage.

Wouldn't you have liked to have known those things when you started?

So share them with people. When you do so, you are not only contributing and paying it forward, you are also deepening the learning for yourself.

When you teach something, you are also rehearsing that principle or practice for yourself. On top of this, you have to have a really good understanding of something to be able to teach it with integrity.

One of the most important things I've done for my speaking practice is to be a speaking mentor and a coach. I mentor for free at my Toastmasters club and I charge for my coaching clients. In both scenarios, I learn so much from the person I am working with. It is through analysing what they are doing and how they are progressing on their journey that I've been truly able to analyse what I'm doing and advance myself.

When you learn things during your speaking journey, pass them on, show others how to learn what you have learned. This is where the real magic of skill development comes from and you will be astounded at how much more quickly you progress when you are doing so.

Develop Your Mastery

I recognise that's a lot of information to take in, so let's recap. The nine principles of mastery are:

Practical

1) Identify: How do you develop your desired skill?
2) Stretch: Challenge yourself just beyond your current capabilities
3) Measure: Find a parameter of progress and record consistently

Psychological

4) Meaning: Know your 'why': why this practice, and the results, are so important to you
5) Aspire: Set high expectations for what you can do and achieve
6) Visualise: Mentally rehearse excellence

People

7) Coach: Find an expert who knows more than you do
8) Peers: Surround yourself with people who promote the skill you desire
9) Teach: Pass your knowledge on to someone else

To turn these principles into practice, I'd like you to get a pen and paper. Look at the items one by one and write down what you are going to do in that area to evolve as a speaker.

Remember to get this as targeted as you can. You can use this multiple times to work through different aspects of your speaking but start with one key area first.

In this first section of the book, you have learned everything you need to begin your Rise.

You have learned how to build your mindset so that you begin seeing yourself as a speaker.

You have learned how to find your message so that you can start reaching audiences as a speaker.

You have learned how to develop your mastery as a speaker so that you can communicate your message more effectively.

This is going to kickstart your journey as a speaker. In the next section, we're going to look at how you really get into the game as a speaker. How do you refine everything you've been learning so far so that you can begin building the foundations of your speaker future?

Section 2: Inspire

"I had two options, one was to remain silent and wait to be killed. And the second was to speak up and then be killed. I chose the second one. I decided to speak up."

"The terrorists tried to stop us and attacked me and my friends on 9th October 2012, but their bullets could not win."

"We survived. And since that day, our voices have only grown louder.
I tell my story, not because it is unique, but because it is not."

(Malala Yousafzai. Nobel Laureate Acceptance Speech, 2014.)

In the last section, you started your Rise. You began to develop the speaker within you. In this section, you are going to learn how to share that speaker effectively with others.

Ultimately, you are only going to be a speaker when you are putting your message out into the world. The behind-the-scenes work is important but you want to be out there on stage, right?

That's what the next three chapters are going to help you do. In the previous section, you learned using the MMM framework. In this section, it's all about your ABCs.

In Chapter 7 **'Audience'** you are going to learn how to reach your people so that you can build a community that raves about you and comes to see you speak again and again. You'll do this by learning:

• The two main types of social media
• Why community is more important than follower count
• The form of digital communication that always works

In Chapter 8 **'Business'** you are going to learn how to monetise your speaking so that you can sustain yourself and reach more people with your message. You'll achieve this by learning:

• To avoid the worse piece of advice in the industry
• How to to build a Rise ladder
• How to get paid for free speaking gigs

In Chapter 9 **'Content'** you are going to learn how to create engaging talks that help your audience implement your key messages. You'll be able to do this once you learn how to:

• Master the most important medium for speakers
• Tell captivating stories
• Use a simple structure to rapidly prepare your speeches

This is where you are going to start seeing your speaking getting put into action. This can be exciting yet daunting at the same time! Stick with it; follow the process and build a bit at a time.

Being an inspiring speaker isn't about jumping onto big stages straight away. It's about doing the groundwork and building the foundations so that when you hit those big stages, you can make the most of those opportunities and create the deepest change you can in your audiences.

Chapter 7: Audience

"To the people of India, whose representatives we are, we make an appeal to join us with faith and confidence in this great adventure. We have to build the noble mansion of India where all her children may dwell."

(Jawaharlal Nehru. 'Tryst with Destiny', 1947.)

If a speaker is on stage and there is no audience, does anyone hear them?

Let's leave that question to the philosopher and make sure you have a captivated audience in front of you when you speak.

You might think that speaking is all about finding people who will position you on ready-made stages in front of already eager audiences. This might have been true before online communication but it's not true now.

Event organisers want to see evidence of an existing audience before they invite you in front of theirs. Why? Because of the incredibly powerful force of social proof.

Imagine you are going on holiday and you are searching for a hotel. You spot two hotels in an ideal location: right on the beachfront, massive swimming pools, and a cocktail happy hour every night.

You see that one hotel has ten reviews, with a 4/5 star average rating.

You see the second hotel has 500 reviews, with a 4/5 star average rating.

Which hotel do you choose?

The second one right?

Why?

Because 500 people can't be wrong.

That is the power of social proof.

In fact, you might go for that second hotel even if the first hotel had a slightly higher rating of 4.2/5 because you trust the judgement of the masses.

The same thing happens in speaking.

If an event organiser is looking at two speakers and one has a social media following of 1000 and the second has a social media following of 100,000, who does that organiser want to be the closing speaker at their conference?

As well as the power of social proof, your audience are your cheerleaders.

They will tell their friends to go watch your videos online.

They will buy copies of your books for their family members.

They will also help you book more speaking gigs. When their child's school needs a speaker, who do you think they will recommend? When their company needs some in-house training, who are they going to refer? When their non-profit needs an ambassador, who are they going to hire?

This is why you can't wait for someone to give you a speaking opportunity out of thin air. You need to earn that opportunity.

Furthermore, let's imagine that I could wave a magic wand and put you on stage in front of 10,000 people. You spend 90 minutes delivering a compelling speech to them and they want to continue to follow you and learn from you.

When they search for your internet presence they find nothing. No email newsletter. No Facebook group. No YouTube channel.

Have you really served those 10,000 people by not having an existing audience that they can join after hearing you speak?

That's why it's important to be building a following from day one. Don't think you should wait until you have the TEDx talk, until you've finished your book, or even until you've done your first speaking gig.

You have to start thinking about your audience now. With that in mind, let's look at the key criteria you need for building your audience.

Choose Your Social

Social media is a double-edged sword. On one hand, it has lowered the barrier for entry for speakers. Anyone with a phone and laptop can get their message out into the world now.

On the other hand, it can be incredibly distracting and overwhelming. You can be so busy making social media posts that you don't do any real speaking.

You do need a presence on social media but you can't let social media get in the way of your speaking.

With this in mind, I want to break down two key functions that social media performs for your speaking.

Broadcasting: Transmitting your speaking to the world
Interaction: Building relationships with your audience

Most social media leans more to one side or the other.

Broadcast platforms include YouTube, Instagram, and TikTok. They allow you to transmit a ton of content but their interaction features are generally limited to commenting on other people's stuff.

Interaction platforms include Facebook, LinkedIn, and Reddit. These allow you to build a personal network and be a part of communities. Although these platforms have broadcast features, they were formed on the foundation of interaction and the broadcasting aspects were added later.

My suggestion is that you need a social media platform that allows you to broadcast and a social media platform that allows you to interact.

The most obvious social media platform for a speaker seems to be a YouTube channel right? It allows you to film all your speeches and stick them on your channel.

But that means you have limited interaction with your audience. You're only ever speaking through the comments section, which isn't conducive for deep connection.

However, if on your videos you say "to continue the conversation with me, you can follow me on Twitter", then that provides people a platform to ask you questions and you can have more of a conversation with your audience.

Some platforms do allow you to do both. I think Facebook is really versatile in this respect. It gets a lot of bad press (rightly so) but its features really are second to none. You have a personal profile to build a network. You have a business page to broadcast information and run ads. You have groups to build a community. You can create events to advertise your seminars and workshops. It really is a one-stop-shop for speakers.

That being said, Facebook might not be the right platform for you. It's about finding the right platform for you and your audience. You might have great success on Instagram: using IGTV to do live speaking; using your feed to post updates and promotional information; as well as utilising the DM function to have conversations with your audience.

We'll return to making your social media decision shortly. Before then, let's discuss the second criteria you need to be thinking of. When it comes to social media, you don't need to just consider the features of the platform, you need to consider user behaviour as well.

Some business gurus will tell you that one of the most important factors to identify is the demographics of your audience: their gender, age, occupation, nationality, political orientation, etc.

When you categorise your audience in this way, that then decides what platform you should be on.

If you work with old male executives, then you should be on LinkedIn.

If you serve 'mumpreneurs' then you should be on Facebook.

If you are trying to reach young people, then you should be on Instagram.

I think this is a strategy that became outdated as soon as the internet came along.

Pre-internet it was true that society would 'congregate' according to its demographics.

Rich and Poor would live in different neighbourhoods.

Old and Young would engage in different activities.

Men and Women would work in different occupations.

The internet broke those traditional silos.

Now Rich and Poor are both watching the same YouTube video.

Old and Young are both in the same Facebook group.

Men and Women are both posting gym selfies.

This isn't to say that there aren't 'trends', it's just that way too much value is put into these trends.

About 80% of my clients are female, so should I start talking about tampons and dresses to 'speak to my demographic'.

About 33% of my clients are people of colour, so should I start appropriating various aspects of their culture to 'speak to my demographic'.

Of course not. In the 21st Century, it is not about demographics. It is about psychographics.

Psychographics are people's beliefs, aspirations, challenges, and behaviour.

I teach people how to find their voice, tell their story, and share their message.

Who, historically, didn't have a voice and is still fighting to have one?

Women and people of colour.

Now, do you understand why my audience looks the way it does?

The demographics are the effect, not the cause.

To bring this back to social media, it is not important WHO is on a platform. What's important is WHY they are there.

For example, do you know what the world's second-largest search engine is after Google?

Is it Bing? Yahoo?

It's YouTube.

When people are searching for answers, YouTube is one of their first destinations.

Think of yourself. If you want to find out how to cook a curry, code a website or choreograph a dance, you try to find a video tutorial, don't you?

After music, video games, and cats, 'how to' is one of the most commonly searched categories on YouTube.

People go to YouTube for entertainment. But they also come for solutions. If you know a common problem that you have expertise in solving, then you want to put that solution on YouTube, as that's where people are looking for it.

The fact that people are using YouTube to search for solutions is a psychographic that you would never appreciate by saying that your market is: "Women aged 30-50 who are married and live in the suburbs of Toronto".

So you want to think of what platform best serves your desired psychographics.

What does your audience believe?
What do they aspire to do/be?

What are their current challenges?

What behaviours do they perform consistently?

Let's illustrate with an example.

A person believes that they are unattractive because they are overweight. They aspire to have a six-pack. Their challenge is that they are unfit and don't know what workouts they need to do in order to get in shape. Their behaviours are buying low-fat options in the supermarket; going into a sports shop to buy workout gear; and buying a gym membership.

What social media platform do you think this person is on?

Notice that I said "a person". Because whether they are male or female, old or young, white or black, gay or straight, Christian or Muslim, conservative or liberal, prefer Star Wars or Star Trek, there's one platform that this person is gravitating to.

Did you guess Instagram?

On Instagram, this person will follow role models who tell stories of how they used to be overweight and unfit and now have the six-pack this person aspires to. They will find videos of their exercises and photos of the meals they eat, complete with recipes in the post description. This person will be able to share their journey on their own profile, their workouts, their meals, and their before and after pictures as they lose weight. The adverts that target them will be for protein supplements and exercise gear.

But Instagram is a young person's platform, isn't it? It's for creatives. It's narcissistic. Surely an old conservative lady won't go on Instagram.

Yes, she will, if that platform gives her the promise of her aspiration and the solutions to her challenges.

That is the picture that psychographics gives you that demographics never will.

So let's bring this all together now.

You need to ensure that on social media you can broadcast and interact. You may be able to do this with one platform, you may need two.

You also need to identify the psychographics (beliefs, aspirations, challenges, behaviour) of your audience and identify what platform(s) they are going to gravitate to.

Let's develop this with a couple more examples.

You want to reach people who believe in doing business differently. They aspire to be able to succeed in a capitalist system and change lives whilst doing it. Their challenge is that they work in an out-dated corporate organisation where profit is always put above the people. They are currently listening to business podcasts, speaking to a career coach, and attending entrepreneur workshops.

What social media platforms are you going to be based on to reach this person? I would suggest:

Broadcast: LinkedIn to post videos sharing your beliefs about 'conscious capitalism' and post articles with case studies of companies that have "paying it forward" as part of their ethos.

Interaction: Twitter to network with 'conscious capitalists' and field questions from your audience.

Instead, let's imagine that you want to reach people who believe that life is all about having fun. They aspire to be able to work around the world and be location independent. Their challenge is that they are trying to find out what occupations would allow them to work short-term contracts and find work in different countries at short notice. They are currently writing a bucket list, enrolled in a photography course, and looking for cheap flights.

What social media platforms are you going to be based on to reach this person? I would suggest:

Broadcast: Instagram to share enthralling stories on IGTV about your fun antics and post pictures of the exotic locations you find yourself in.

Interaction: Facebook where you create a group where you and the other members can share job opportunities, travel deals, and 'best practice' for working and living in different countries.

Now try that for yourself to identify what platforms your audience are going to be on and how you are going to connect with them.

<u>Build A Community</u>

This leads on somewhat from the previous segment.

One of the things you need to be careful of with social media is 'vanity metrics'.

These are big numbers that don't equate to tangible impact.

100,000 likes on a post… so what? People just click the thumb and scroll on by.

10,000 followers… so what? 90% of them will unfollow you if they don't see that you are following them too.

There are people with 1M followers on Instagram who are broke because they have a faceless following rather than an engaged audience.

There are people who don't even have a social media account who are making a real difference in the world.

Social media activity and a following is good, as long as it is coming from an engaged community and not browsers.

With this in mind, I have two suggestions to help you foster a community spirit.

Create A Meetup Group

One of the most versatile instruments in your arsenal as an emerging speaker is meetup.com. This site is a hub for groups and events in cities and towns across the world. Since COVID-19, you can also use it to find and host online events.

On Meetup, you select a list of interests, and it provides you with a list of Meetup groups holding events that match your selected interests. These include big topics like health, literature, and business.

However, these groups can get really specific and niche. Do you like board games? There's a Meetup group for that. Do you like '90s Trance music? There's a Meetup group for that. Do you like playing board games whilst listening to 90s trance music? There's a Meetup group for that too.

Meetup can be used to network and find opportunities to speak on other people's stages. If you are speaking on exercise and nutrition, you can attend exercise and nutrition Meetups to find partners and clients.

However, if you also host your own exercise and nutrition Meetup then partners and clients come to you. That for me is the real power of Meetup. On Meetup, people have already self-selected their interests and already self-selected to join your group and come to your event. They are receptive to what you have to teach them.

You can join Meetup for free to attend events, however, to host a group larger than 50 people (Which is nothing on Meetup. Most groups are in the 100s if not 1000s.) you have to pay for at least their first level subscription. This works out at about $15 a month and I'd consider it to be the most effective form of paid advertising there is. To put this in perspective, it takes me about $30 worth of Facebook advertising to get ONE person to sign up for a free event. With Meetup, I can get about 20-30 people to sign up for a free event.

So sign up for Meetup and create a group. As you begin your journey, keep your group name general. This is all about exploring who you are as a speaker, what type of student is attracted to you, and ultimately who you really want to serve. For example, my first Meetup group was called "Growth Group" as it was all about personal growth. If you were teaching marketing in London, you might call your group "London Marketers".

Ironically, advertising to a general audience is normally terrible marketing advice. However, you aren't marketing the finished product, you are developing the finished product. You are throwing mud at the wall and seeing what sticks. You want to attract anyone who is remotely interested in marketing and start seeing who shows up and finds what you are talking about useful.

The next step is to start holding events. You can hold all sorts of events on Meetup. You can create socials, networking, classes, workshops: anything that brings people in your group together. You can run these for free to try and get as many people through the door or charge a small price for them to cover any costs you have, it's up to you.

You will notice that your group grows at a healthy rate, especially if you have a general sounding name. People can sign up for as many groups as they want, so if your group has the slightest appeal to them, there's a good chance they will sign up. You can amass hundreds of members in a very short time and even grow your group into the 1000s.

This of course does not mean you will get thousands or even hundreds of people signing up for your Meetup. In fact, most of your members will never sign up for an event, and even less will take the further step of attending.

What is powerful about this feature of Meetup is that you can market to all of these people. If "London Marketers" has 500 members, and it schedules an event, all 500 of those members are sent a notification. Next, that event is marked in their Meetup calendar as something they can attend. You have just reached 500 people, interested in marketing, without spending a penny.

Furthermore, there is a feature where you can email all the members of your group. I'll talk about creating a proper email list later in the chapter, but this is a great way to notify hundreds and even thousands of people in your group that you are running an event.

I like to use Meetup as the first entry point for people into my work. It works for me and it can work for you too. Use Meetup to get used to running regular events, building your audience, and training your speaking ability.

As you continue to do this, you will start to gain greater clarity on what exactly you are offering as a speaker, and who wants it. Eventually, the time may be right to hone and specialise that Meetup group.

As you continue running events for "London Marketers", you may notice that you enjoy speaking to digital marketers most and that you seem to get a sizeable proportion of marketers working in hospitality. Therefore, the name might change to "Digital Marketing for Hospitality". You may see the overall growth and size of your group decrease, but the actual audience at your events becomes more tailored and specific to what you want to talk about. In this scenario, you've used Meetup as a testing ground, and now it's helped you gain clarity on your audience and your message.

Online Group

As well as having the in-person Meetups, I also recommend giving your audience a place to hang out online.

Online communities, when done correctly, can foster strong feelings of connection. They are not only a great supplement to in-person meetings, they also allow you to reach and serve people beyond geographical limitations.

You have a couple of different options for an online community.

1) Facebook Group

Facebook groups are the most obvious and accessible. Groups are fairly versatile and Facebook is actively pushing them at the time of publication. Since most people have a Facebook account, this is a low barrier of entry.

Facebook groups allow you to post pictures and videos, poll your audience, and create events for the group. The options truly are extensive.

Equally, you have to be aware of the potential limitations of a Facebook group.

The first is the mass of distractions on Facebook. Your group has to compete with all the usual noise on Facebook. It also has to compete with the other groups too. Because Facebook groups are versatile and easy to create, everyone is making one. What will make your group stand out from everyone else's?

Linked to this is dead engagement. If your group doesn't get regular engagement, then it is dead in the water. I'm sure you've been in groups where the host is just speaking to themselves. They post a video and nothing happens. They have regular posts like "Motivation Monday" or "Win Wednesday" that week after week don't interest people enough to engage. You can't build a community around one person's monologuing.

I'm sure you've seen the exception to this though. If there is a post like "Promo Thursday" or "Selling Saturday" then suddenly a bunch of people comes out of the woodwork to spam the group. That's not a community interested in collaborating and connecting.

If you do create a Facebook group, then you have to protect it. Firstly, you have to protect it from yourself! Resist the urge to just use a Facebook group as your own personal echo chamber. Yes, post helpful content and even be the 'main' voice in the group, but you need to make sure you are giving a voice to your members too. This can be achieved by using devices like polls, interacting on Facebook Live, and giving them the opportunity to post questions and discussion prompts.

Secondly, you have to protect it from bad apples. Bad apples will rapidly kill the culture and suck the engagement dry. Bad apples try to position themselves into groups and promote themselves. As soon as you see this behaviour, kick them from the group. When you allow these bad apples to accumulate, your group will turn rotten.

If you avoid these pitfalls, you can have a thriving Facebook group that allows you to have an engaged following across the world.

2) Mighty Networks

Mighty Networks is a group-specific platform designed around community building. Mighty Networks offers the same versatile features that Facebook does: videos, polls, discussions, etc.

The advantage of using a platform like Mighty Networks is that it removes the distraction of Facebook. Your members log in because they want to engage with your group. They are not randomly browsing and checking in like they do with Facebook.

On the flip side, had you heard of Mighty Networks before reading this book? Probably not. Because it is not a regular platform, it requires that your members very quickly get into the habit of logging into this unfamiliar platform to engage with your group.

If not, then you are quickly going to suffer the curse of dead engagement.

3) Video Meetings

A different method of building a community is to have regular video meetings with your audience using technology like Zoom. This could be weekly, fortnightly or monthly sessions where you run a networking event, group activity, or Q+A session.

With this method, your audience gets to see and speak to each other in a fashion similar to being in the same physical location. This is fantastic for connection and community building.

This approach definitely requires the most time and effort on your part to make it work, so you have to be careful that doing this isn't detracting from your main focus: speaking.

When you have established a social media presence and begun to foster an emerging community, you are then ready for the next step.

Email List

Bringing your audience together in an email list is vital. Since the internet's early days, email has always been the most direct channel of communication to people.

But what about Facebook/Twitter/Instagram/TikTok/next new social media?

For all those social media platforms, what do you need to input to create an account?

Your email.

Email is still the best place to get close to people.

Firstly, a social media platform can change its algorithm and totally wreck your ability to reach your audience. Facebook and Instagram both used to have incredible reach until they became ad-driven platforms. Currently, TikTok is deliberately giving you unnatural organic reach to get you hooked onto the platform (one of my friends recently got 100,000 views on a post with just 100 followers). Watch TikTok monetise that and take away the reach in the next 3-5 years.

Email will always be the same model: sequential messages in. No one can pay to have their emails take higher priority. It's a level playing field.

Secondly, email feels more intimate. Social media will always have a 'speaking to the masses' element to it, even when you use quite specific language in your posts. Email feels more like someone writing directly to you, even though you know it's a mass email. There's even software in email marketing platforms that allow you to insert the person's first name into the text. Again, you know it's software when you receive it, but you still feel the validation of being addressed by name.

Thirdly, people are more likely to buy through email. If you are selling books, tickets to your events, online courses, or coaching/mentoring programs, you will make few of those sales through social media. People don't make large purchases on social media. This might seem odd given the number of ads on these platforms but if you click on some of these ads you are seeing, you will notice that most are actually offering a free gift, free trial, or small low-cost item. What details do they want you to provide to get this low-cost offering?

Your email. That's when they are going to sell you the bigger stuff.

The key to being a successful speaker over time is to build this email list. When you write a book, the subscribers to your email list will be the first ones putting in the preorder (I recommend all speakers write a book. It's why I've written this one!). When you announce an event, they will snap up the early bird tickets. When you are looking to work closely with a small group of clients, they are going to be your best candidates.

What do you need to use to create an email list? You can't do this just using your Gmail account. You need an email marketing platform to store the information safely and to provide some of the advanced tools you will require (scheduling emails, signup forms, A/B split testing, etc).

There are a number of great platforms out there. I would always recommend starting with Mailchimp. Mailchimp is free for your first 2,000 subscribers and is relatively straightforward to learn. You are welcome to research alternatives though.

How can you grow your email list? I have three suggestions.

1) Ask

The first method is not complicated. Just ask people if they would like to be on your email list. This is how I got my first 8 email subscribers!

Send out regular emails to your contacts and post on social media asking for people who would like to join.

Whenever you are speaking at an event, have a signup sheet or a laptop/tablet where people can provide their details if they would like to continue to hear more from you.

This doesn't bring in a large number of subscribers but it does bring in some of your most active subscribers. Because these are people who you have personally asked, generally they have a closer relationship with you and wish to actively stay in touch with you.

2) Free Gift

This is the traditional model of building an email list. You will see this all the time.

'Receive this free PDF'

'Download this free guide'

'Sign up for this free webinar'

You've clicked on these tons of times before, haven't you?

You exchange your email for a free gift. Generally, you are then placed into an automated sequence that builds more of a relationship with you, shares some more information then sells you something.

This model is effective, but I do have a few issues with it.

Firstly, it's a little tired. As soon as I see that word 'free', I know I'm going to be put into one of these sequences, and I can't really be bothered getting the extra volume in my inbox. When you've been through a few of these you know that the free information usually isn't very helpful because they are aiming for the big sale at the end.

Secondly, there's a lot of unethical practice in these sequences. They tell you to quickly sign up for a free 'live' webinar (It's not live) because there are only a limited number of spaces (there aren't). Then there will be a lot of predatory, manipulative language designed to put you in a bad emotional state and make you feel you 'need' what they are about to sell you. Then they slam you hard with the sale: 'this is half price for a limited time" (no, they always sell it at that price), the offer expires in 20 minutes (no, it doesn't), there's a limited number of products available (no, there aren't).

None of this is to say that you shouldn't use this model. There is nothing wrong with the model, it's the way it's often used. When you use this model, be helpful. Offer a free resource that's going to genuinely help people get started.

Also, be honest. If you are going to offer a live webinar, make sure it's live. If you are only going to offer ten places on a course so that you can work closely with each person, don't sell an eleventh and twelve place to make an extra buck.

This model works, I would just ask that you have some integrity using it.

3) Showcase Event

I have developed a third approach to building my email list, partially because of my gripes with the 'free gift' model.

This method is by far my most successful and is responsible for the vast majority of my email subscribers.

I don't offer a free gift, but rather a free event. Usually in-person, but I have expanded this to online events too as my business has grown.

People sign up for the event using their email. I then provide them the details of where they can join me live ('real' live, no pre-records or holograms!).

Then I spend a short amount of time, 1-2hr, running a small workshop for them.

I teach them real stuff, none of the motivational fluff that is normally on these 'free webinars'.

Sometimes I will offer something for sale, sometimes I don't.

The main purpose of this event is so that people get to meet and experience me and start to build a relationship before they find themselves on my email list.

This method requires a little more work than the 'free gift' model, but I think that effort pays off.

As a speaker, I don't think you can hide behind automated email sequences and prerecorded training forever. Such mechanisms do have their place and it's the only way to really scale your work. You can't deliver a workshop every day or you will burnout.

However, I love the advice of the founders of Air BnB: Brian Chesky, Nathan Blecharczyk, and Joe Gebbia. They say that sometimes you should do things that don't scale.

When they started Air BnB, they personally went round to their hosts and took professional photographs of the properties. It made Air BnB look attractive and safe in the beginning when one of the concerns they had to address was their customers' fear of where they might be staying.

They aren't going around and taking professional photographs now but that early action set the standard for when the business did scale.

Running countless free events doesn't scale. You can't run events all the time and you also need to run events that people are paying for to sustain yourself. Nonetheless, this 'showcase event' is a fantastic way to bring in engaged email subscribers, especially when you are starting out as a speaker.

Grow Your Audience

In this chapter, you have learned how to build a loyal, engaged following who are going to be your greatest supporters and cheer-leaders.

Firstly, you learned how to choose social media platforms that are right for you and your audience. This ensures that you can broadcast to, and interact with, your audience without being over-whelmed and spread too thin over unnecessary platforms.

Secondly, you learned how to build a community. You learned the importance of creating an in-person community and an online community.

Thirdly, you learned the importance of ensuring your following are subscribed to your email list so that you can develop a closer relationship with them. You learned three different ap-proaches that you can use to grow your email list.

Your audience is your lifeblood. If you don't have an audience, you aren't a speaker!

You need to be able to sustain yourself as a speaker, otherwise, you aren't going to be able to get your message to all the people it needs to reach. You need to approach speaking as a business if you are going to succeed. You are going to learn how to do so in the next chapter.

Chapter 8: Business

"Now ordinary people have voice, not just those of us lucky enough to go to HBS (Harvard Business School), but anyone with access to Facebook, to Twitter, to a mobile phone."

"This is disrupting traditional power structures and levelling traditional hierarchy. Voice and power are shifting from institutions to individuals, from the historically powerful to the historically powerless, and all of this is happening so much faster than I could have ever imagined when I was sitting where you are today and Mark Zuckerberg was 11 years old."

(Sheryl Sandberg. Harvard Business School Address, 2012.)

You have to approach speaking as a business.

There's no other way to say it.

If you don't, you are never going to make the impact you are capable of.

To truly get your voice out there, you don't want to be worrying about rent, food, and looking after your family.

Speaking needs to provide your shelter, sustenance, and a whole lot more.

Income is necessary to advertise your message to more people, host big transformational events, and hire awesome people to help you.

If you keep on doing free gigs for the Rotary club then you are stunting your ability to make a difference to people's lives.

I'm not having that on my watch.

Therefore, this chapter is all about how you monetise your speaking.

Don't worry, you are not going to need a business or marketing degree to understand this chapter.

To be honest I don't want to overwhelm you and make you feel that this whole speaking thing is more than you signed up for.

Instead, I want to provide basic foundations and principles that you want to be thinking about as you begin your journey as a speaker.

By all means, get those free gigs in the Rotary club, that's all part of the journey.

However, what you're going to learn in this chapter might help you cover your petrol money for that gig, and perhaps buy yourself a celebratory meal afterward.

Tantalised?

No?

What if I told you that you could be making enough to cover the travel to *any* Rotary club in the country and dine at the finest establishment in that town?

Now we're talking.

Let's find out how you can make this happen.

Don't Quit The Day Job

This is probably the most important piece of advice I'm going to give you in this book. It's a huge myth that I think needs to be debunked and so many so-called 'influencers' bang on about this from the safety of their social media feeds.

There is this insidious idea that to be a real entrepreneur you have to "go all-in", "burn the boats" and "escape the 9-5".

Guess what happens when you go all-in? You lose your chips and you are out of the game.

Guess what happens when you burn the boats and find out you're on the wrong island? You're stuck there.

Guess what happens when you escape the 9-5? You swap eight-hour workdays for sixteen-hour workdays.

When I first started, I was listening to all these 'hustle' podcasts and following 'motivation' accounts on Instagram. The message I was hearing, again and again, was that you aren't a 'real' entrepreneur unless you are working on your passion full-time.

So, after I attended Experts Academy, I decided it was time for me to go "all-in" on my dream. My future wife and I moved to another city, and I decided this was the perfect time to "make it happen".

Of all the times to "go-all in", doing so after you have just moved to a new city, in a new country, isn't the time to make it happen. I had no base, no contacts, no audience, no revenue, and no clue. I quickly wiped out my savings and realised that I was not going to "make it happen". I had to scramble around for a job whilst my mum paid for my rent and my future wife bought me food. Some 'motivational speaker' I was.

When you first start as a speaker, you are going to be making a net negative. You're going to be traveling to free gigs and networking. You're going to be hiring rooms to host workshops. You're going to be paying for professional training and coaching. You aren't going to see that money coming back when you first start speaking. If you don't have an existing income to carry that, you're going to find yourself in trouble quickly.

You won't be able to get your name out there with free events and create connections. You won't be able to take risks and try something new with your events. You won't be able to invest in your development. As a result, you play safe and you play small.

Worst of all, you are going to stop thinking about service and start thinking about money. You lose your drive behind your speaking and start doing anything to make a quick buck. If you lose your 'why' behind your speaking, the quality of your speaking will suffer. If your speaking is poor, you certainly aren't going to get paid for it.

Instead, use your job as a springboard for your speaking. If you have a regular income, you can afford to travel and take advantage of great opportunities that perhaps don't have an immediate financial outcome. If you have a regular income, you can pay for venues and build your experience as a seminar leader without having to worry about your bottom line. If you have a regular income, you can invest in training for your speaking (such as this book!).

In the early days, your speaking will be a net-deficit, and you will need to support it with your job. Eventually, your speaking will start to be a net profit, which is very exciting. I still encourage you to keep your job in this scenario. Why?

When you have an alternative source of income, it means that all your profits from your business can be reinvested back into your business. You can buy equipment, marketing, and training to further improve the business. The business starts to feed and nourish itself.

However, if your business is your only income, then the profits don't go back into the business. They get stolen away by your landlord, the taxman, and the supermarket. Your business is being used for bare sustainability and survival, not for growth and creating a life of service and impact.

When I first moved to that new city, I 'hustled' and 'grinded' and managed to organise my first full-day event. I got 16 people in the room and made £600 in a single day. This was great, but I had spent four weeks utterly focused on that event. That was my entire month's earnings. My rent at the time was £437. My bills were about another £100 on top of that. Most of that £600 got sucked into keeping a roof above my head, leaving me with some spare change to buy food for a couple of weeks. My business didn't see any of that hard-earned money.

I had to shift my mindset towards a job and see it as a gift to my business, not a burden. Having a job facilitated the growth and development of my business, not hindered it.

I was lucky enough to get a job in a school during this period and it was the perfect job for my progress at the time. I got to work with disadvantaged students and I learned a lot about psychology from working with them. Working with them gave me practice and experience in mentoring and empowering. I worked 9-3 and left my work at work. It gave me enough money to sustain myself and I got evenings, weekends, and school holidays to work on my craft.

I also enjoyed my job, which is a rarity among the people who attend my seminars. Generally speaking, I didn't come home in the evening moody and irritable. I got on well with most of my colleagues. I got to do some fun activities and go on some interesting school trips. I didn't long for the weekend and spend my Saturday and Sunday exhausted.

Eventually, I became frustrated and recognised that I was in danger of getting stuck there. I realised that I needed to move on and make the jump to start speaking full-time. However, I made that decision after I had been there for two years and I devised an exit strategy to help me make that transition.

I would recommend finding a job like this for yourself if you aren't in one already. Four key criteria will allow you to find a job that supports and enhances your business. You want a job that:

1) Provides you with some form of experience relevant to your speaking (e.g. working in a marketing firm to teach you marketing skills you will later use in your business).

2) Provides you with a good amount of free time to work on your craft (e.g. working three 12-hour shifts in support work to give you four free days).

3) Provides you with a good income to supplement your business (e.g. working some form of corporate role).

4) Provides you with good networking opportunities (e.g. working in events management and meeting people who might hire you as a speaker in the future).

If your job ticks at least one of these criteria, then it is going to add something to your business whilst you are still building it and setting the foundations for the transition to being a full time speaker.

I hope I have convinced you in this part of the chapter to stick with your job. Don't believe all this influencer bullshit that you aren't doing it right unless you pack it all in and start living life by the seat of your pants. It's far smarter to develop multiple sources of income to give your business the foundations that will eventually give you the means to springboard into doing it full-time.

How do you start to develop these multiple sources of income? How do you start to bring in some speaking income to supplement, then replace, your job income? That's what you are going to learn next in this chapter.

The Rise Ladder

As a speaker, you are going to take your audience on a journey. You are going to take them from where they are now to where they want to be.

You'll do this at the micro-level with every speech you deliver. Each speech your audience hears moves them a little further along their journeys.

You'll also do this with the way you set up your business. Your business is set up in a way that takes your audience on a journey. Your products and services that you charge for are positioned at different points along this journey.

We can view this journey like a ladder. It looks something like this.

Product 4: $$$$
Product 3: $$$
Product 2: $$
Product 1: $

What does this mean? You are creating a journey for your audience where they get better the furthest they climb up the ladder, you work with them more closely at each rung of the ladder and you charge more to rise to the next rung. We're going to illustrate this with two wildly different examples.

Amber is an ultramarathon runner and personal trainer. She speaks about developing her confidence through fitness after being bullied at school.

Marcus is a lawyer for Small and Medium Enterprises (SMEs) who speaks about his journey of fighting injustice and racism as a black person in a white neighbourhood.

Let's go through each rung one by one to explain how it works and we will relate it back to Amber and Marcus at each point.

Product 1: $

Information Product
Low Price
Minimal Involvement

Your first product is designed to get your audience started on their journey.

You want to give them relevant, useful information that doesn't overwhelm them.

You want this to be a low price so that anyone can access it.

You also want to have minimal involvement, so that you can scale it to lots of people.

The ideal product to start the ladder is a book. It's why I believe every speaker should write a book (I keep on recommending it don't I? You'll start seeing why as we continue).

A book is a great way to give your audience information and ideas to get them started.

A book is within everyone's price range.

A book takes a little bit of time to write but after that, you are done. You don't need to keep on updating it to sell it to people.

Before you panic, this doesn't have to be a book, I just think that is the best option.

This could be a downloadable PDF with market trends for different social media to help people with their marketing.

This could be downloadable MP3 files with meditation tracks for anxiety reduction.

The key aspect is you create the information once and you can keep on serving people with it.

It allows people to get in the game and learn the basics. That's the key point though: the basics. You don't give them all the advanced, juicy stuff at this stage.

Firstly, you're going to seriously undervalue your expertise.

Secondly, your audience isn't ready for it yet.

You can't throw your audience in at black belt level, you've got to start them off at white belt level.

Whilst there is a huge temptation to give your audience everything at once because you want to help them, they actually can't deal with it.

That's why you've got to make this a journey for them. Let them get their white belt first, then you can take them to the next step.

Let's return to our examples of Amber and Marcus to see how they approach this.

Amber decides to create a recipe book tailored towards endurance athletes called *Fueldurance*. She prices this at $19.

Marcus decides to create a downloadable white paper outlining the ten biggest legal mistakes that SMEs make. He prices this at $7.

Let's look at how Amber and Marcus's Rise Ladders start.

AMBER	MARCUS
Fueldurance Recipe Book: $19	*10 Biggest Legal Mistakes* White Paper: $7

Amber and Marcus both have a starting point for their audiences. Amber doesn't want to throw her audience into a 100km run and Marcus doesn't want to throw his audience into a 100-page legal document. They start them off gently and then can build from there.

Product 2: $$

Information Product
Medium Price
Marginal Involvement

Your first product is designed for your audience to be able to dip their toe into the water.

Now you want to help them swim.

You're going to give them further information.

You're going to ask for increased financial investment.

You're going to be more hands-on during the process.

For these reasons, I recommend that product 2 is a subscription or membership. This is important for two reasons.

Firstly, it tests people's commitment. Are they going to put in the time and energy to learn what you have to teach them? Are they going to come back week after week or month after month?

Secondly, it provides you with reoccurring income. It's income that you can rely on each month. Even if it isn't enough to sustain yourself fully in the beginning, it gives you a foundation to build on.

There are two main models for this approach.

I classify the subscription model as paying to have something sent to you regularly. For example, think of subscribing to a magazine that gets delivered through your letterbox once a month. This doesn't have to be a physical product though. For example, you could email someone a new training video every month.

I classify the membership model as paying to have access to something consistently. Think of having a Netflix account and being able to watch anything, anytime.

The key aspect is that your audience is paying a little bit of money to engage with what you've got to share consistently.

This means that you can gently introduce them to more information without overwhelming them.

It also allows them to sample more of what you're about and see if it's really for them.

I bet you have subscribed to a couple of things and realised they weren't for you.

By the same token, how long have you had your Netflix account now?

If your audience likes what you do, they will stay with you for a while.

To return to our martial arts analogy, they have made the decision that they want to have more than just a white belt.

Let's return to Amber and Marcus to see what they decide to do here.

Amber creates a 12-month workout plan called *The Ultra Blueprint*. When her audience subscribes they get sent a new 4-week workout plan every month, along with instructional videos demonstrating how to perform the exercises. Amber has minimal involvement as all she needs to do is create the workout plan and videos each month then upload them to the subscription site. She prices this at $47 per month for their 12-month subscription.

Marcus creates a member's hub called *SME Solutions*. Members of the hub receive access to a variety of useful legal resources. In addition, Marcus runs a monthly webinar series where he outlines the latest legal developments concerning SMEs. He speaks live for one hour on this webinar, and then fields 30 minutes of questions at the end. After uploading the resources, Marcus's only involvement is this 90-minute webinar each month. He prices this at $97 per month.

Let's return to the Rise Ladder and see how this is filling up for them.

AMBER	MARCUS
The Ultra Blueprint Workout Plan: $47/month	*SME Solutions* Members Hub $97/month
Fueldurance Recipe Book: $19	*10 Biggest Legal Mistakes* White Paper: $7

Now Amber and Marcus are starting to serve their audiences on a more consistent basis. It is also giving their audience time to connect more with their work and who they are. The key aspect is that they are still able to scale this to a large number of people with minimal involvement from themselves. It also gives them the stability of regular income, which gives them a foundation to produce more advanced products, like the next two we are going to discuss.

Product 3: $$$

Mass Service
High Price
Close Involvement

After your first two products, your audience is ready to decide whether they are serious or not. Do they enjoy having a weekly spar in the martial arts class, or are they keen to go for the black belt? Both are fine, but by this point, you have made the distinction.

At this point what you are offering starts to take on a distinctly different look. You go from a product (a thing they can use) to a service (you are doing it with them) and the focus changes from information to implementation.

Your involvement with the audience becomes much higher and that is reflected in the price that your audience now pays.

You only have so much time, energy, and attention to give. You can't give everything to everyone, so you have to be selective. You have to ensure you are working with the people who are going to most benefit from hearing your message and are committed to making the change you can provide for them.

The two best ways of doing this are either an online course or a live event. Through these two mediums, you can give your audience advanced knowledge, along with the tasks and activities required to implement that knowledge.

With an online course, you can film training videos, have downloadable worksheets, have a Facebook Group where the members can talk to each other, and host live Q+As with yourself using Facebook Live or Zoom.

With a live event, you can get people together in a room to talk and work together. You can teach and demonstrate things from the stage. You can get them to engage in individual reflective activities. They can also engage in partner discussions and group activities.

Let's look at how Amber and Marcus set this up for themselves.

Amber creates an online course titled *12 weeks to Marathon* designed to get people from a standing start to running a marathon in three months. In this course, she provides short instructional videos, downloadable training logs, and a Facebook Group for members to share their training. She also does a live video in the group every week called "Motivational Monday" to set the students up psychologically for the week ahead. She prices this course at $297.

Marcus hosts a weekend conference titled *SME Summit* which brings together a variety of legal experts to make sure owners of SMEs are protecting themselves from every angle. This conference has a selection of keynote speakers (of which Marcus is one) as well as several smaller breakout sessions and networking breakfast, lunch, and dinner. He prices a ticket for the conference at $777.

When we plug these into the Rise Ladder, this is how it looks.

AMBER	MARCUS
12 Weeks to Marathon Online Course: $297	*SME Summit* Conference $777
The Ultra Blueprint Workout Plan: $47/month	*SME Solutions* Members Hub $97/month
Fueldurance Recipe Book: $19	*10 Biggest Legal Mistakes* White Paper: $7

Both Amber and Marcus now have an elevated offering where they can take their audience deep and start to work with them in a much closer way. The audience will definitely notice the shift between the first two products on the ladder and Product 3. Equally, they are ready for it because they've taken the journey to get to this point. If they are willing, they can also take the journey a step further.

Product 4: $$$$

Individual Service
Very High Price
Intimate Involvement

Now it's time to work with the black belts.

When your audience gets to this stage, they are ready for mastery.

They have changed a lot thanks to you, now they are eager for fine-tuning.

You're going to be working very closely with them now. The investment you will be making in them is reflected in the financial investment they now have to make.

At this level, you are going to be working either with a small group or individually.

The terms 'coaching', 'mentoring', 'consulting', etc., are often used interchangeably and are defined differently by everyone. Rather than discuss their nuances I will use the term "coaching" from this point on to capture any work you do at this rung of the ladder.

Coaching looks very similar whether you do it with an individual or a group. You meet regularly: weekly, fortnightly, or monthly. The sessions usually last 60, 90, or 120 minutes. You work together for an extended period, generally 3-12 months.

The difference is that with group coaching you get the added benefit of sharing ideas and expertise with the other members in the group, with a trade-off of slightly less one-to-one time with you as their coach.

Let's see how Amber and Marcus add this last item into their Rise Ladder.

Amber creates the *Marathon Mastermind*, a three-month group coaching program. This is where she works with clients who have run a marathon and now want to train for ultramarathons. She meets up with these clients in person, planning their routes, leading the runs, and cooking meals with them. To join this Mastermind for three months requires an investment of $2500.

Marcus offers his consulting services for a year. He will work with the CEO of an SME and provide legal counsel when required. To hire Marcus for a year in this role requires an investment of $10000.

Amber and Marcus's Rise Ladders are now complete.

AMBER	MARCUS
Marathon Mastermind Group Coaching $2500	*12 Month CEO* Consultancy $10000
12 Weeks to Marathon Online Course: $297	*SME Summit* Conference $777
The Ultra Blueprint Workout Plan: $47/month	*SME Solutions* Members Hub $97/month
Fueldurance Recipe Book: $19	*10 Mistakes* White Paper: $7

Now that we've worked through all the Rise Ladder, let's take a breath and clarify a few things. Firstly, you do NOT have to create all these offers overnight. If you try to write a book, create a course, and take on coaching clients overnight, you're going to get overwhelmed. The Rise Ladder is just to show you what you are building towards. It takes time.

As I write the Rise and Inspire book (this is product 1 I'm sure you have realised) I don't have the full Rise Ladder in place yet. But I know that will come when the book is finished.

Secondly, don't get overwhelmed by these prices. You might be looking at Marcus charging ten grand and thinking *"how the hell can I charge that much?"*. These prices are a guide to give you an idea of scale. The dollar signs give you a rough idea of how many numbers should be in the price. Marcus doesn't charge $7 for his consulting but he also doesn't charge $10000 per month for his members hub.

You can even scale this down and simplify this at the beginning with just three products.

You could have a subscription for $9 per month. 100 subscribers would bring in $900 a month.

You could have an online course that costs $50. Ten new students per month would bring in $500.

You could charge $100 an hour for your one-to-one time. You could have a weekly meeting with one client. That would bring in $400 each month.

With those three offers, you now have $1800 a month coming in.

That isn't much to live on, but it's a start, isn't it?

Now that you've seen the maths play out, you've realised why you need to charge more than that as time goes on though, haven't you?

Again, don't get overwhelmed with this right now. Start with ONE offer that you think would best serve your audience right now. Would you like to document your incredible personal story in a $12 book? Can you set someone up in 5 simple steps in a $197 online course?

Your Rise Ladder will extend over time and act as a structure for what we're going to talk about next.

Free vs Paid

One of the biggest decisions you will find yourself making over time is whether you speak for free or get paid to speak.

Naturally, everyone will want you to speak for free. Naturally, you want to be paid to speak.

Here's the golden statement when someone is inviting you to speak.

"My speaking fee is X, does that fit your budget?"

You will get one of two answers.

1) "Yes, that does, are you available to speak?". In the rare situation you get that response, you know you're speaking with a pro.
2) Stammer/stutter/sharp intake of breath/silence followed by "Oh, we weren't expecting to have to pay you". This is the response you will generally get; especially at the beginning of your speaking journey.

So, do you simply proceed with the paid gigs and ignore the free ones?

Not necessarily.

Free gigs can still be highly lucrative.

Why?

Because you have a Rise Ladder.

Your Rise Ladder gives you the means to make money from a 'free gig'.

Your Rise Ladder is your secret weapon as a speaker.

Whilst you've got the other person stammering and stuttering at the other end of the conversation, you can follow up.

"Since you don't have a budget for speakers, can I suggest an alternative…"

"…I have a bestselling book on blahblahblah, would I be able to sell and sign copies at your event?". At every event I've ever done, free or paid, I've been able to sell my books.

"…I have an event coming up soon that I think would be useful for your audience, would I be allowed to promote it at the end of my talk?". I sell tickets for paid events at free talks and webinars.

"…this event sounds like it will have my ideal clients attending. Would I be able to give out my details for them to contact me about my services?" I meet the vast majority of my coaching clients through my free Facebook Group.

What often happens is that the event organiser feels guilty about not being able to pay you, so they are happy to make the concession.

Now you have a decision to make. If you feel you can sell enough books/tickets/sessions to make it worth your while, then you can accept the gig and perhaps even make more money than if you'd just charged your speaking fee.

If they say that you can't sell anything, then you are just doing a freebie. Unless this is for a charity cause you care deeply about, or it would provide you with great exposure and credibility (like a TED talk), then kindly decline, stating that you are a professional speaker, so you can't do freebies. Honestly, if you start doing free gigs because you're desperate, you'll only make it harder to find anyone willing to pay you.

Sadly, I have to say this, but I see it too often not to mention it. Some organisers will try to get you to PAY for the privilege of speaking. I once got offered a 20-minute slot at an Expo for £3500! In this scenario, tell them to fuck off in as diplomatic a fashion as you wish.

Build Your Business

When you felt that call to become a speaker, you perhaps didn't anticipate that you would have to approach it like a business.

What I hope to have demonstrated in this chapter is that, although you didn't anticipate it, creating a speaking business doesn't have to be scary or complicated.

Firstly, we firmly dispelled the myth that you need to quit the day job to begin your journey as a speaker. You need the stability of your job to feed what you do as a speaker.

Secondly, we looked at how you construct a Rise Ladder, creating a journey that your audience will take with you and earning you money in the process.

Thirdly, we examined the Free vs Paid debate and saw that doing a free speech doesn't necessarily mean that you don't earn any money if you can promote products and services that you have from your Rise Ladder.

That's all you need to know to get started. You have the basics required to start earning money as a speaker. When you do, you support yourself so that you can serve others to a greater degree.

In this Inspire section, you have learned how to grow your audience and build your business. Now it's time to learn what you're actually going to say to them. How do you create compelling content that will inspire your audience to make the transformation you desire for them? That's what you're going to learn in the next chapter.

Chapter 9: Content

"Immaculate Heart High School, graduating class of 2020.

"For the past couple weeks, I've been planning on say-ing a few words to you for your graduation.

"And as we've all seen over the last week, what is happening in our country and in our state and in our hometown of LA, has been absolutely devastating.

"And I wasn't sure what I could say to you.

"I wanted to say the right thing and I was really nervous that I wouldn't, or that it would get picked apart, and I realised the only wrong thing to say is to say nothing."

(Megan Markle. Immaculate Heart High School Graduation Speech, 2020.)

There is one equalising factor amongst all speakers.

Let's face it, some speakers are born attractive, which makes them more inviting. (Did you know that the most physically attractive political candidate usually wins? Think Kennedy vs Nixon)

Some speakers are born taller, which makes them look more commanding. (Again, the tallest political candidate usually wins. Consider Reagan vs Carter)

Some speakers are born with 'charisma', that oozing confidence and gift of the gab that draws people's attention. (No surprises now, the most charismatic political candidate usually wins like Obama vs McCain)

You might feel you are not born with such advantages, but there is a way that you can not just level the playing field, but gain a massive competitive advantage.

It's through creating a massive amount of content.

It's through putting your voice out into the world again and again.

How many sermons do you think Martin Luther King had delivered as a reverend before he stood up for 'I Have a Dream'?

How many cameras do you think Ronald Reagan stood in front of as an actor before he stood in front of a camera and said "Mr. Gorbachev, tear down this wall"?

How many lecterns do you think Barack Obama stood at as a lawyer and lecturer before he stood at the lectern to deliver his Presidential Acceptance Speech?

These speakers had put a vast library of content out into the world long before they stood to deliver their most famous and historically significant speeches.

Content is the great equaliser among speakers. The more you put out there, the better you'll get and the more influential you will be.

Learning how to create content is an absolute necessity as a speaker. Every speaker does it in their own way and you will find your way too as you develop.

What you're going to learn in this chapter is the basics of how you create and present great content.

Video Is Key

I know your hands are going to squeeze tighter on this book or ebook reader you are holding. You're going to scrunch your eyes in despair. You might even let out a groan.

You're going to react in this way because I'm telling you that if you want to be a speaker, you need to get onto video.

You need to start recording yourself speaking. Not only that, you need to be posting these videos online.

I can feel you cringing from here but you need to snap out of the resistance you might be experiencing.

If you want to be a speaker, then you need to speak and you need to expose yourself to audiences.

If you can't do that with a phone camera and social media, how do you expect to be able to do it with a stage and rows of eyes staring at you?

If you aren't comfortable hearing yourself speak, why would you expect anyone else to be comfortable hearing you speak?

If you can't expose yourself to a couple of passive viewers on YouTube, how do you expect to expose yourself to hundreds of active listeners in a conference room?

Additionally, learning to speak on camera is vital so that you can jump on the rising tide of virtual speaking: so that you can do Facebook Lives, run Zoom webinars, and be a keynote speaker at virtual conferences.

When people tell me they want to be a speaker, this is the first and only piece of advice I give them. It quickly separates the wannabes from the real deal. If someone isn't willing to record a five-minute video and post it to their 53 followers on social media, I know they haven't got the desire required to be a speaker.

Recording videos was what Brendon Burchard urged me to do…and I did it. I didn't procrastinate by buying fancy cameras, mics, and lights. I sat in front of my laptop, turned the webcam on, and spoke into it. That was it. I recorded the speech in one take and posted it on my Facebook.

In my first video, I spoke about the importance of journaling. I spoke about how it was helping me deal with the emotions and grief of my recent loss of Dad to cancer. I spoke about how you could blog as a creative outlet. I spoke about keeping a gratitude journal and the benefits that had for happiness.

The speech was not polished, it was not rehearsed. I ummed and ahhed. I repeated myself. I touched my face nervously. But I did it.

I was surprised when that video got over 300 views on Facebook and about 15 likes. People didn't care whether it was polished or professional. They just cared that I was speaking about something that mattered and they could resonate with and learn from.

That positive reaction was certainly good encouragement to keep on recording videos, but I would've still filmed the next one even if it got 10 views and 0 likes. I was going to be a speaker and I was going to do whatever it took to make it happen.

That video is still on my YouTube channel. It is my very first video, entitled 'How journaling helps you deal with negative emotion'. You can go and watch it if you like. I leave it up there to show people to start before you feel ready and just get in the game.

Since recording that video, I have recorded a video every single week, generally varying from 10-25 minutes.

Every single week, for the past five years at the time of writing this book. That's over 250 videos. If you record 250 videos, I guarantee you will be a better speaker.

I posted each one of these videos. I knew I wasn't a speaker if I didn't have an audience. I admit that I have deleted some of them. Not because I'm ashamed of my beginnings, but because the quality was so poor I don't think people got value from them. I rambled, repeated myself and didn't articulate points clearly.

But it didn't matter.

I needed to do these rambling, shockers of videos to develop into the speaker I am now. And you need to do the same to become the speaker you are capable of being.

Before we even talk about the mechanics of doing these videos (which to be honest, there isn't much of), I want to get you in the right mindset to do this. If you have resistance to this, then you have resistance to being a speaker, and you need to smash right through that.

Firstly, video makes you self-conscious. I get it. You think your face looks like you've had a stroke. You say the word "like" in every second sentence. The camera lens stares you down like the Eye of Sauron.

What you've got to remember is that your audience's inadequacies matter more than yours.

Your audience is struggling with challenges in life. They're struggling with their weight, their mental health, their finances, their sex life, their spirituality, whatever area it might be in which you are trying to help them. They're searching for answers. Answers that you might have.

And you're not going to give them those answers because you feel self-conscious?

You've got to realise that your mission is more important than you. The game is so much greater than the player. You are the player and you need to get in the game.

Here's the truth about starting. You have all these fears about people's judgement. You're worried they're going to think you look stupid. You're worried they're going to think you're speaking rubbish. You're worried you're going to be a magnet for trolls and cyber-bullies.

Oh no no no. This is not what will happen at all.

Something worse will happen.

People won't care.

People won't care that you're filming videos. They are too busy worrying about what they're doing to worry about what you're doing.

People won't care that you're posting on social media. You will sit on the sidebar of people's YouTube accounts. They will scroll past you on the Facebook feed.

There's only one thing worse than being criticised: it's being ignored.

And that is what you've got to look forward to in the beginning.

So if people are going to ignore you, what's the point in feeling self-conscious? You aren't going to get subscribers and you aren't going to get views when you first start, so use this time productively.

Use this time to actually start getting good at video and public speaking. Monks go into solitude to practice their meditations. Be a monk and use this solitude to practice your public speaking.

As you keep posting videos, eventually, you are going to pick up some scraps. People will come across you randomly or keep seeing your videos and finally decide to tune in for once.

In the beginning, you aren't going to pick up the haters. Haters don't care when you're starting. Haters don't hate obscurity because they're not jealous of it. Haters only pay attention when you're successful because then you start to trigger their inadequacy. Quite frankly, if you aren't posting videos because you're worried about the haters, then you have delusions of grandeur.

What comes first are the supporters. The people who take time out of their day to give you some attention. The people who give you a cheeky 'like' (probably after only watching 43 seconds of the video, but you don't need to know that).

Bit by bit, the followers and subscribers stay. You don't have to keep refreshing your page to get the views into double figures, your audience really is that size.

Do you know why that audience begins to accumulate? Because by that stage, your videos actually have some value. You're more confident, competent, and concise. People are genuinely enjoying watching your videos and get value from them, because you took all that time to practice when they weren't looking.

So how can you build this competency? I have a few guidelines to help you in this process.

1) One Take

Turn the camera on, start speaking, and keep speaking until you have reached the end of what you want to say. A lot of people get stuck on messing up in the first ten seconds, get self-conscious, and start again. The camera starts rolling, they flub another line and it's back to the beginning again.

If you do this, then you are not giving your speaking space to develop. You're stopping before you have even got started. It's like deciding that you want to start running and stopping the first time you get out of breath.

Keep the camera rolling. Speak through the mistakes. Correct yourself and move on. Don't let the first hundred metres stop you from completing the race. Get to the end, then you can edit out the mistakes. You can cut out rambles, you can join up points, you can clear up hesitations and memory blanks.

This of course means you need to learn a little bit of editing or know someone who can edit your videos for you. I get iMovie with my Macbook, and the Apple techies have shown me enough basic skills to allow me to do any edits required, although that is rare because of the next skill I encourage you to learn.

2) No Script

One of the most important skills you can learn to be a speaker is to be able to speak without a script, either in hand, on a podium, or memorised. Academics and politicians speak from scripts, and neither of these are good examples of inspiring speakers. You can get away with any speech up to about 60 minutes using a memorised script, but beyond that, you going to struggle to be able to speak from memory alone.

One of the key skills I encourage in speakers is to stop speaking from the head and start speaking from the heart. That's because we don't connect head-to-head, we connect heart-to-heart.

When you speak from the head, you are having to think too hard about what you're doing. You're trying to remember what you should be saying right now. You're planning what you should say next. You are too focused on yourself and not enough on your audience. It's a terrible way to communicate.

When you are having a conversation with someone, do you have to 'remember' what to say to them? No, you just say what comes to you at that moment. Do you have to 'plan' what you are going to say next? No, you just follow the flow of the conversation.

When we have a conversation, we are speaking from the heart, and the heart has no memory. You don't need to endlessly practice and memorise every conversation you have before you meet someone, you just speak to them in that moment.

The heart also has no fear. The heart is actually the opposite of fear. It is where courage comes from. We don't say "They had the head of a lion" or "they showed a lot of head to keep going" do we? When we speak from our head, we allow our fears, doubts, and insecurities to creep into our speaking. When we speak from the heart we speak from a place of courage and power.

When we use scripts, we are training ourselves to speak from the head. You will never be a truly inspirational speaker if you speak from the head. When we don't use a script, we are training ourselves to speak from the heart.

When you record a video, decide what topic you are going to speak on, or a question you are going to answer. For example, you might decide to record a video on "Why you should eat Gluten-free" or "How to be more productive".

When you have your topic, then think of three to five points you are going to talk about. For example, if I was to make a video about how to look good on video (videoception) then my three points would be:

1) Eyes
2) Hands
3) Smile

What you do with these three things dictates how good you look on camera. I would go into the video with just those three points in my mind, and then riff on them.

This might seem intimidating.

"How can I remember what to say using just three words?"

"How can I share enough about those three things without doing research?"

You have far more expertise in your subject than you give yourself credit for. If you were sitting at the bar with a friend and they asked you a question about your expert subject, I'm sure you could start rattling off statistics, stories, and strategies. If you can do that with a friend at the bar, why should it be any different speaking to the camera?

Decide on your topic and what your main points are going to be and then just start speaking about them. If you make a mistake, lose your place, or forget something, then as we covered in the last point, speak through it.

Imagine that your video (and your speeches when you come to do them) is a journey, and these main points are landmarks along the journey. You want to hit all of them, but there isn't a prescribed route to take. You don't have to take the main road and it doesn't matter if you take a wrong turning. Just keep making your way until you hit that landmark. When you've hit one, work your way to the next. That journey might be a little smoother. You might decide to take a tangent and add in an extra landmark.

That is the joy of speaking in this way. You aren't fixed to a single route that you have to hit perfectly, which is what happens when you are speaking from a memorised or written script. This is difficult to do in the beginning but it's the only way to develop your long-term speaking abilities.

3) Watch it back

You've reached the end of the video. You ummed and ahhed and floundered and wandered, but finally, you said your piece and were able to end the torture.

Well, now you've got to go back into the dungeons and put the thumbscrews on again.

It's time to watch your performance back again.

When you first start, this will be agonising. Within the first 60 seconds alone you will pick up on several annoying mannerisms and tics you have.

"There I go, scratching my chin for the fifth time."

"There I go, not pronouncing my "T"s for the eighth time."

"There I go, giggling nervously for the two hundred and sixty-third time. Hehe."

These are frustrating to hear, especially when they seem so obvious now but you were completely clueless as you repeated them over and over.

Don't be disheartened by these. We all have these little tics and mannerisms, even in everyday conversation, never mind the increased pressure of public speaking. Even advanced speakers are still identifying and cutting out little tics. Sometimes we develop new tics and have to weed them out too.

The important thing is by identifying them, you can then do something about them. However, trying to take on all your tics at once is challenging. Instead, work on them one at a time. If you have counted a hundred and twenty-four "ums" and "ers" in your video, then next time, focus on just taking a silent pause when you are thinking of your next thing to say. When you have taken these filler words out of your speaking, then focus on your complete lack of facial expression or how you finish every sentence on a high pitch like it's a question...?

If you want to become a speaker, then the consistent filming of videos is one of the most valuable things you can do for your development. It is the closest simulation of being on stage, and you can do it far more often and easier than trying to source live audiences to speak in front of.

Signature Story

The first speech you should develop, before anything else, is your signature story.

Your signature story forms the backbone of everything you speak about.

It also gives you something to speak about, even when you have NOTHING to speak about!

For the first two years of my speaking career, pretty much all I spoke about was my story of losing Dad to cancer and the three lessons I learned from it.

It's how I first built my reputation as a speaker because everyone who heard the story then wanted me to tell the story somewhere else.

You will always have speaking opportunities if you can tell a good story.

What we've got to work out for you is what your signature story is.

Because you might be thinking *"I don't have an amazing story to tell"*.

Believe it or not, that might be a good thing.

The more amazing the story, the less relatable it is to your audience.

In 1969, the Astronauts came back to Earth to tell us about the Moon Landing.

An incredible tale of adventure and ambition, but how relatable is it?

We haven't been on the moon and probably can't grasp the intensity of the training and engineering involved to make it happen.

In 2003, Aron Ralston was canyoneering in Utah when a dislodged boulder pinned his arm to the canyon wall. Stuck there for five days, Aron escaped by amputating his arm with a pocketknife. He then rappelled a 20m drop and hiked 11km to safety.

Ralton shares this story now as a motivational speaker. Don't get me wrong, this is an incredible story of human courage and determination.

It's not very relatable though is it?

How many of us have been in the situation where we've even considered sawing our own arm off?

The more incredible the story, the less relatable it becomes.

There's a power in simplicity.

I didn't appreciate until I started telling it how relatable my story was.

Losing a parent is a natural process. It's something that we should, in the natural order of things, all experience.

Cancer is also a common experience. With cancer rates now one in two, just about everyone has lost a loved one or knows someone who has.

I could get people in the audience nodding "me too" and they would often come up to me afterward and tell me their similar story.

That's the reaction that you want because it shows you are connecting with your audience.

So how do we work out what your signature story is?

Your signature story is why you are reading this book.

What made you want to become a speaker? Why do you feel you have a message to share with the world? How do you feel uniquely positioned to help others?

Your signature story is likely the defining moment of your life. Here are some 'generic' stories I hear all the time.

"I saw a fat holiday picture and realised I needed to lose weight. So I started running. On my first run I was out of breath by the time I got to the end of the street, but I knew I needed to keep going. I was able to complete my first 1K, then my first 5K, then my first 10K. I started to enjoy

the buzz and the progress I was making. I'm now a marathon runner and personal trainer. "

"I burned out in my corporate job and realised I was in the wrong career. I waited until my next quarterly bonus and then handed in my resignation. Everyone told me I was crazy and after several months all I'd done was eat into my savings. However, a journey to South America opened my eyes to some of the social issues I knew nothing about and I felt a call to volunteer in this community. This brought me a sense of purpose and contribution I had never felt in my corporate role. I now run a non-profit helping children in Bolivia."

"I was a single mum working three jobs and realised I didn't have the time to spend with my children. So on my night shift job, I started to moonlight with an online Shopify account. For months I was losing money on it but eventually, I managed to get it profitable, which allowed me to quit two of my jobs. I kept on building it up until I was finally able to quit the third job. The sense of freedom I felt and the ability to truly connect with my children was amazing. I now work my own hours and get to prioritise time with my children over time at work."

All of these stories are fairly relatable, aren't they? Does one of them describe you? Or perhaps someone close to you?

Do you also notice that these stories follow a pattern?

Storytelling is a fine art and I could write a whole book about it whilst still exposing my ignorance of how much I've still to learn about it. To keep things simple for you, allow me to share the Simple Storytelling System. It's the structure you see in each of the stories above.

1) Struggle (Why)
2) Search (How)
3) Solution (What)

Let's break down what's happening at each of these points in the story.

Struggle: WHY

You have to start with struggle for two reasons.

Firstly, it makes you relatable. I know you've seen a speaker who's started something like this:

"I worked at < insert household company > for ten years. As Vice President of Sales, I increased our revenue by < insert ridiculous percentage >. Last year I was awarded the < prize you've never heard of but apparently is a big deal >."

On a scale of not impressed to not impressed, how not impressed are you?

It's not that achievements aren't inspiring. It's just that leading with them at best lacks the context necessary to understand them and at worst makes you look like a raging narcissist.

You need to demonstrate that you are a real person, with warts and flaws just like everyone else.

The second reason is that you need to start painting a journey for your audience.

Remember you aren't speaking to people who have got their life figured out. In some way, they are struggling and you've got to show you understand that struggle because you've been in the trenches yourself.

Furthermore, you need to show them that there is a path out of that struggle.

That is why your story starts in the same place theirs does, so that they can see this journey is possible for them too.

When you start with struggle you are sharing why the audience should listen to you.

As Simon Sinek says: "People don't buy what you do. They buy why you do it."

Look at those examples I gave above and look at how they start:

"I saw a fat holiday picture and realised I needed to lose weight." (*I know what it's like to not take care of yourself, have low self-esteem, have something sneak up on you, feel disgusted, etc etc*)

"I was a single mum working three jobs" *(I know what it's like to have to stretch money out to make it last, to be meeting yourself coming out the door, to choose between feeding your children and feeding yourself, to have the insecurity of having a vital source of income taken from you at any moment, etc etc)*

They start with a story that is common and relatable. Most importantly, it starts in a place of struggle, not success.

This is where your story starts too.

What is your struggle that your audience can relate to?

Search: HOW

In the previous step, two important things happened:

1) The audience related to you
2) The audience saw their story in you

What this means is that the audience is now ready to follow you on a journey. They know it's a journey that they want to go on and they trust you as their guide for this journey.

You are now going to outline that journey. You identified a problem, that was your struggle. What did you then do about it?

As their guide, you need to warn them about the hurdles and the false summits. Don't pretend this is easy, because it's not. Equally, help them keep the faith that progress can be made.

What you are starting to do is outline the steps the audience needs to take from where they are, to where they want to get to. They may have taken a few of these steps already, but at some point you are going to get ahead of them and be showing them the path up ahead.

Once the audience recognise their struggle in you, they are now looking to you for answers. The tricky thing is that if you tell them the answer straight up, they won't get it. They will see it as too detached from their current reality.

That's why this step is all about signaling HOW they are going to overcome their struggle.

Let's see how this was done in the examples above:

"So I started running. On my first run I was out of breath by the time I got to the end of the street... (*I started from the bottom*)
"... but I knew I needed to keep going... (*I persevered even though it was tough*)
"... I was able to complete my first 1K, then my first 5K, then my first 10K." (*I gradually got better*)

"I waited until my next quarterly bonus and then handed in my resignation. Everyone told me I was crazy... (*I know what it's like to go against the status quo. I know what's it's like to have to convince people you're doing what's best for you. I know it's tough going up against opposition*)
"... and after several months all I'd done was eat into my savings... (*It didn't work out for me immediately. I had to be patient. I had to consider that perhaps I had made the wrong decision*)
"... However, a journey to South America opened my eyes to some of the social issues I knew nothing about and I felt a call to volunteer in this community." (*I kept trying until I found something*)

Do you see how the stories shift from the struggle into a search? The overweight person tries running. The corporate burnout quits their job.

The next key factor is that this part of the story shares some of the challenges that you encountered on your journey and, by extension, your audience is likely to encounter as well.

It's important to highlight these challenges because you are showing HOW you overcame them.

The first part of your story is telling people why they should listen. The second part of your story is showing how they can learn from you.

What are the steps you took to escape your struggle and what are the challenges you faced that you need to make your audience aware of?

Solution: WHAT

As you take your audience on this journey, they are going to hear of how you overcame challenges and moved on from your struggle.

They're now getting excited because they can see themselves in your story and wonder "could I do this too?".

This is when you show them the possibilities. You show them the result of your journey. The good stuff that you worked hard to get.

This is when you get to list the accomplishments, titles, awards, and whatever else you have gained from your journey.

At this point though, it doesn't have the self-serving vibe that it does when you lead with this information. Why? Because you aren't really talking about yourself (or you shouldn't be).

You are actually talking about your audience.

This is the tricky part to understand with a signature story. It's not actually about you.

Your story is really about the audience seeing themselves in you.

When you list your accomplishments and successes at the end of your story, it is actually about showing your audience what is possible for them, not about putting yourself on a pedestal.

If you put yourself on a pedestal, you'll fail, because your audience will think "well that's all right for them, but I could never do that". They shut themselves off from the destination because you didn't do a good enough job of showing them the journey.

As a speaker, you are a leader. It's not about getting yourself to the destination. It's about getting others there with you.

Let's look at how this plays out in some of the sample stories:

"This brought me a sense of purpose... (*desired outcome*)
"... and contribution..." (*desired outcome*)
"... I had never felt in my corporate role..." (*acknowledgement of improvement*)
"...I now run a non-profit helping children in Bolivia." (*change in circumstances*)

"The sense of freedom I felt..." (*desired outcome*)
"... and the ability to truly connect with my children was amazing." (*desired outcome*)
"I now work my own hours..." (*change in circumstances*)
"... and get to prioritise time with my children over time at work." (*change in circumstances*)

Hopefully, you will see a pattern in how you finish your signature story (if you don't, then I haven't followed my own mantra and led you to the destination!).

The audience doesn't want your accomplishments.

They want to know what will be different in their life by following you to that destination.

They don't want to run a non-profit, they want to know that they are doing something purposeful and meaningful.

They don't want to have a Shopify business, they want to have freedom from worrying about money and time to spend with their children

Additionally, they want to know that the journey they are on will lead to these payoffs. They want that sense of finality (even though everything in life is an ongoing process). They want the story to end, like all novels, films, and TV shows eventually do.

The result is arbitrary. Your audience will tell you that they want to run a marathon/quit their job/start their own business but that's not what they truly want!

They want some fundamental human needs met and they want a sense of having completed their own story. The accomplishment is just what they associate with those desired outcomes.

The Solution is all about showing your audience WHAT they can get but not in the way that you think. You have to make the desired outcomes and conclusion of a journey clear to them before you outline that your accomplishments were a vehicle that allowed you to do so.

What outcomes have you reached that your audience will also find desirable?

That's the entire system.

To recap:

Simple Storytelling Structure (SSS)
1) Struggle (Why)
2) Search (How)
3) Solution (What)

Your signature story takes time to piece together. Even if you know what it is right now, it will take time to craft and sculpt into a story that takes your audience on a journey, rather than just describing your life.

When you've nailed it though, it's one of the most transformational tools you will ever possess as a speaker.

Speech Prep

In your journey to becoming a speaker, there's one thing you're going to be doing a lot of.

Speaking.

When you get your first gig, you will get super excited and spend weeks, maybe even months preparing it (I know I did!).

Then you will get another and spend weeks preparing that.

Suddenly, as the gigs start to increase, you realise you can't spend as much time preparing them.

Your prep work has to get much faster.

You need to find a system that works so that you can recycle existing content for new audiences or create new content at times.

You are welcome to spend the time in the trenches finding your own system the tough way.

Or you can just use mine.

What I'm sharing with you here is my Perfect Preparation Plan that you can use for ANY speech.

I've used it for everything from my seven-minute wedding speech to my two-day weekend event.

Here's the outline, we will explore it in more depth below:

1) Parable (Story)
2) Point (Message)
3) Practice (Action)

Part 1: Parable

We just talked about the importance of having a great signature story in the previous segment. As we dissected that you could see why stories have such a powerful effect on our audience.

Starting with a story is the easiest way to begin a speech. It is low risk, high reward. It's pretty hard to butcher a story (although I have seen it done!) and if you tell it well you will have your audience captivated and listening to everything else you have to say.

We've just outlined the Simple Storytelling Structure that will help you tell an awesome story, so we won't go into too much extra detail here.

What I will outline are examples of the types of stories you can tell.

A personal story often works, which is what your signature story is. However, it doesn't always have to be about you.

You could highlight a case study from your industry.

You could describe a client's experience.

You could narrate a historical event or person.

You could even make up an actual 'parable' like *The Good Samaritan*.

If you're playing it safe, the easiest stories are about you or a client you have worked closely with. Stick to them if you're not sure.

The rare times I've seen stories crash and burn are when people try to get fancy with them. They create a convoluted parable or try to be poetic and get words to rhyme. If your audience thinks you are trying to be fancy, they will feel you are trying too hard and will be put off.

Stories should be simple, don't overcomplicate them.

Step 2: Point

Although stories are the low-hanging fruit of public speaking, that doesn't mean that you won't encounter a thorn from time to time.

Remember that the story is a tool to communicate some kind of message.

You're not on stage to tell your audience a bedtime story.

Your story has to have a point to it.

This is where the framework goes slightly out of order.

Although you tell the story first in your speech, you have to know the point before you choose what story to tell.

You identify what the message of your speech is, then you pick a story that best illustrates that.

You don't say "I fancy telling the audience a story about a hare and a tortoise racing, that will be entertaining and I hope they get something from it."

You say "I want to tell my audience today about the importance of consistency and perseverance. What's the best story that illustrates that? The parable of the hare and the tortoise."

Do you see the difference?

You plan what the point of your speech is first, then you lead with the story that best serves that point.

Step 3: Practice

Near the beginning of my speaking career, I didn't know what I was doing.

Then I went to a seminar where the speaker told me the secret to being a successful speaker.

Be confident.

Thank you so much for reading this book, you've been a great audience.

Wait, what?

Did you feel that something was missing there?

What did you expect to find out, then not find out?

How to be confident, right?

This might seem like an exaggerated example, but I see speakers do this ALL the time.

They tell a little story (usually about themselves) then give some advice that you could find in thousands of fortune cookies or Instagram quotes.

Then they just walk off the stage, thinking they've done their job.

As a speaker, you are a leader, and it is your responsibility as a leader to provide direction. You've got to help your audience make the progress they desire. It's not enough to tell them what to do, you need to show them what their next step is.

There's nothing wrong with the fortune cookie philosophy or Instagram platitudes, wisdom is pretty timeless.

However, you've got to back it up.

You've got to show your audience how to put your Point into Practice.

This simply involves highlighting the next step, or the next couple.

Maybe you have a tool they can use (e.g. if you want to get started filming video, get yourself a Manfroto tripod, you can take it anywhere, and it stops you from getting a sore arm recording selfie videos all the time).

Maybe you have a technique they can try (e.g. when you walk onto stage, stand and pause for several seconds before you start speaking, it makes you look more confident and draws the audience's attention).

Maybe you have a framework they can use (e.g. when planning your speech, use the Perfect Preparation Plan. Haha, see how it works now?).

You've got to give your audience something they can take away from your talk. That's how they will remember you. That's also why they will want to come back and see you again and again.

That's the formula. Pretty simple right?

To recap:

Perfect Preparation Plan (PPP)

1) Parable (Story)
2) Point (Message)
3) Practice (Action)

Once you've used this a couple of times, you'll start doing this automatically.

You might be wondering, is this it? Can I really make a speech that lasts an hour using this? Or a workshop that lasts an entire day?

Probably not, but there's a simple way around this.

You just repeat the formula.

When you've told a story, made a point, and outlined a practice; then just tell another story, that makes another point and has a practice.

I told you this was simple, didn't I?

Over time you will develop extra little nuances within each area, but this structure still works even when you get to advanced levels of speaking.

Create Your Content

It's taken some time to get here, but now you're finally putting out content as a speaker.

Your success as a speaker will be determined by the quality of the content you put out there and this chapter is designed to help you get that quality up to scratch quickly.

Firstly, you learned how to train yourself to speak confidently on video in three simple steps. Being able to speak effectively on video allows you to reach people anywhere in the world.

Secondly, you learned how to construct a powerful signature story using the Simple Storytelling System. Your story is one of your most powerful means of inspiring people.

Thirdly, you learned how to structure any speech using the Perfect Preparation Plan. This allows you to get ready to speak fast so that you can get on as many stages as possible as a speaker.

I know we've done a LOT of foundational work to get you here, but a building's height is determined by the depth of its foundations.

Your Rise as a speaker will launch in proportion to how much investment you make into these key fundamentals.

Creating content is fun. Enjoy the process and the journey. The quality won't be as high as you'd like in the beginning but that's okay. Commit to the process. The more you do it, the better you get at it.

That's the underlying message that I hope you have picked up from this book: the more you speak, the better you'll get.

What I hope to have done so far is to have given you some processes that will help you on that journey.

Let's cover one final thing, shall we?

Conclusion: Encore

"I have led you into history. I leave you now to make new history."

(Betty Friedan. Farewell speech as first president of the National Organisation for Women, 1970.)

I remember the evening I finished my first full-day seminar. I felt tired physically but invigorated spiritually (and I dislike using that term, so it shows how powerful the feeling was!). I felt that I had found my calling.

My now-wife and I got home and I gave her a big hug in the kitchen.

"This is the beginning," I whispered to her, "this is where it all starts."

When I said that, I was both correct and incorrect.

That was indeed my first signature event and I've done many since. From that perspective, I was correct.

What I really meant when I said that, however, was that I had done the hard work. Now I was going to run event after event and it was going to grow and scale into something glorious purely because I had pushed over the first domino.

From that perspective, I was utterly wrong.

I had done a lot of preparation for this event. I had constructed and delivered to a high standard but I had missed one important factor.

Beginner's luck.

If you have ever read *The Alchemist* by Paulo Coelho, you'll know that the protagonist, Santiago, is constantly tapping into the force of beginner's luck. In the book, beginner's luck is described as "the force of the universe that pushes us down the right path". If we didn't have beginner's luck giving us that initial burst of motivation in the beginning, we'd probably never get to where we're meant to be.

It's quite likely that you will notice things go well in the beginning. You record a video that gets quite a lot of views. You run an event that a large number of people sign up for. You ask for a paid speaking gig and you get it.

What you may notice afterwards is that it can be harder to follow that up.

The video views go down. The attendee numbers drop. The paid opportunities dry up.

This is okay. This is because beginner's luck got you inspired; now you're being tested to see whether you're really prepared to choose this as a path.

This is not to dissuade you, it is to prepare you. You are not yet the finished article as a speaker.

You will get worse before you get better.

It will get harder before it gets easier.

There will be failure before there is success.

This is the nature of the journey you are now embarking on.

It is not easy to speak up and be heard in a world full of noise.

It is not easy to rise to your feet in a world where people are criticised for taking a stand.

It is not easy to inspire a world where so many people are feeling uninspired.

It is your duty, however, to be a voice.

I believe that we all have a voice and we all have a message that should be heard.

You have to fight for that message, and fight to make it heard.

This book was written to help you do that.

I wrote this book to help you get your voice out into the world, to help you to begin your journey as a speaker.

However, I must leave you to make this journey yourself, at least for a little while.

I can't tell you what that voice should sound like, what it should say, and who should hear it.

That is for you to find.

With this book, I hope to have sparked the magic of Beginner's Luck and send you down the path you are destined to tread.

All those years ago at Experts Academy, I made the decision that I was going to move and inspire someone the way that Brendon Burchard had moved and inspired me.

I hope that perhaps that person is you.

I hope that I have awakened the voice within you.

Now go out and make that voice be heard.

It's time for you to Rise and Inspire.

Stay In Touch

This might be the first time that I've spoken to you but I certainly hope it isn't the last. I've been waffling on for a fair while now, so I'd like to give you the opportunity to make your voice heard. Below are a couple of suggestions for how you can do so.

Rate And Review

Audience feedback is vital to the work we do as speakers. I'd love to hear what you thought of the book. Please head to Amazon and leave a rating and review so I can find out how it was for you.

Digital Contact

I'd love to stay connected with you on the speaker circuit. I've included all the options for how you can stay in touch below.

- Website: www.riseandinspirespeakers.com
- Facebook Group: Rise and Inspire Speakers (RAIS)
- Youtube: David McCrae — Virtual Speaking Coach
- Linkedin: David McCrae — Virtual Speaking Coach

Acknowledgements

She appears under several different monikers in this book as she has been a part of the journey from the beginning. Whether she has been my girlfriend, partner, fiancé or wife, Kerrie has always believed in me, even when I didn't believe in myself. When others might have said "stop trying" or "be more realistic" Kerrie has always said "how can we make this work?". It is her faith in me that has helped me develop into the person I am today. I couldn't have done any of the things I have been able to achieve without her. I'm grateful for her ceaseless love and support.

There is so much to thank our parents for, starting off with our very existence. I always try to acknowledge my parents in a different way in each of my books and with this book I think it's appropriate to acknowledge their contribution to my speaking.

I'd like to thank my dad, Jim, for playing Wayne Dyer tapes in the car when I was young. Just listening to those tapes probably planted a seed deep in my mind that it was possible to be a speaker.

I'd like to thank my mum, Sarah, for taking me along to the radio station. There was a time when she had a regular segment on local radio and I would sit in the studio and listen to her. Watching my mum speak so confidently to a live audience was fantastic modelling that I could one day do the same.

As well as my biological parents, I would like to show my gratitude to my parents-in-law, John and Katrina. They are actively involved in my life and projects and always show interest and encouragement in what I am doing. They provide support to my wife and I in a myriad of different ways and I'm deeply appreciative of it.

I would like to acknowledge some of the speaker role models who have inspired me to greater heights with their words. The first, who has featured heavily in this book, is Brendon Burchard, who changed my life from stage. The second is Barack Obama. I remember running home from school so that I could watch his Inauguration Speech in 2009. He was the first political leader who inspired me. The third is Simon Sinek. He is such an articulate speaker who always shares such insightful perspective. I have a lot of time for him and always seek his viewpoint on important issues.

I have been lucky enough to have many mentors closer to me in life than these role models. These include Lauren Robertson, Ehab Hamarneh, Bob Train, Carolyn George, Jo Richings, Dan Gregory, Ash Phillips, Francis Ghiloni, Karen Yates and Wendy Li. Each of these individuals have given me a lot of their time and expertise and I appreciate that they were willing to invest this energy and attention in helping me become a better person.

I'm grateful for the friends I have in my life including (but not limited to): Josh, Andy M. and Lauren, Owen, Jamie C. and Roz, Jamie W. and Sarah, Andy S., Ruaridh and David.

Every time I write a book, I'm grateful to all the people who help me proofread and provide feedback. For this book I would like to acknowledge the efforts of: Roz, Laura, Dave and Angela F., Angela V., Tom, Stuart G., Kit and Stuart D.

I would like to acknowledge the work of Mercedes Pinera for the cover design. I found it difficult to think of a way to convey public speaking in a way that was clear but not cliched. I would like to thank her for her patience as I put her through a LOT of variations before she found the magic with this one.

Finally, and no less importantly, I would like to thank YOU the reader. I appreciate not only that you've read this book, but that you've read all the acknowledgements filled with a lot of people you don't know. In the end, it's you as the reader that keeps us authors going. Thank you for taking the time to trust in this book and in me as its author.

About The Author

David was born in Aberdeen, Scotland, to an English mum and a Scottish dad. He jokes that this makes him a Half-Blood, just like Harry Potter. He was raised in the village of Banchory just outside Aberdeen. Arguably the village's biggest claim to fame is that the Queen of the United Kingdom drives through it every time she stays in her Balmoral Estate in the Cairngorm National Park.

David was a nerd long before it was cool to be one. David has watched the Lord of the Rings films over 100 times and used to own a replica sword from the movies, which will naturally be replaced with a lightsaber when they get invented. David knows, as any intelligent person does, that Han shot first.

After growing up in Scotland and watching the Lord of the Rings on repeat, it's unsurprising that David has developed a fondness for mountains and is currently working his way through the Scottish Munros: the 282 mountains over 3000 ft tall in the country.

David is a long-suffering fan of Scottish Rugby. Every year he sits down eagerly to watch the Six Nations Championship and hopes this year will be the year that Scotland win their first title (they're getting closer!).

David also has a minor obsession with cats. He speaks to the cats in his neighbourhood and has assigned them all names and personalities. Some of the cats reciprocate his attention. All of his neighbours give him a wide berth.

David likes to consider himself a "Pun Master". He knows the double-meaning of far too many words and will jump upon any opportunity to showcase that knowledge. His personal favourite is when he went to a restaurant and a waiter greeted him with a tray of drinks.

"Aperitif?" the waiter asked.

"No thanks," David said, pointing to his mouth, "I've already got a set."

Printed in Great Britain
by Amazon

15735067R00092